Fall in Love with the Whispers of Your Heart

A guide to transformation from the inside out

Dear Catherine,
Blessings on
your journey
within. ♡
With Love,
Ann ♡

Ann Ruane

Published by Ann Ruane

Copyright © 2020 Ann Ruane.

Published by Ann Ruane

All rights reserved. No part of this book may be used or reproduced by any means, graphic, electronic, or mechanical, including photocopying, recording, taping or by any information storage retrieval system without the written permission of the author except in the case of brief quotations embodied in critical articles and reviews.

Because of the dynamic nature of the Internet, any web addresses or links contained in this book may have been changed since publication and may no longer be valid. The views expressed in this work are solely those of the author.

The author of this book does not dispense medical advice. If medical or other expert assistance is required, the services of a professional should be sought. The intent of the author is only to offer information of a general nature to help you in your quest for emotional and spiritual well-being. The author and publisher specifically disclaim any liability that is incurred from the use or application of the contents in this book.

Paperback and eVersions of the book are available at:
www.LuxEternaHealing.com/books

ISBN: 978-1-09832-661-6

Printed in the United States of America

Art and Graphic design by Tracy Delfar

Author photograph by Jamie Healy, The Native Dreamer

FIRST PAPERBACK EDITION

To all courageous souls
with an insatiable curiosity to
become aware.

With Heartfelt Gratitude

Fall in Love with the Whispers of Your Heart was nurtured, supported, and enhanced by a few beautiful souls. A special thank you to the following people: Tracy Delfar, whose inspired art and vulnerable connection to her gift graces every page of this book, from the cover down to the layout; Jamie Healy, whose infectious joy for her gift of photography invited an introvert like me to be captured naturally in front of her lens; Mike Boutott, whose quiet presence and commitment to family shared his editing skills and encouragement; Carol Dusold, whose unwavering friendship and support created a safe space to process the journey in addition to making the time to edit my work; and to my husband Mike Ruane, whose love and support helped make this book possible.

Foreword

Healing is balancing energy. Ambika Wauters, author of *The Book of Chakras*, states, "We are a complete energy system that unites all levels of being into an energetic totality. What we think and feel influences every cell in our body. It contracts or expands our energy field and stimulates our vitality and the amount of resilience we have at our disposal."[1] All of the thoughts and feelings that we keep to ourselves or attempt to push away impact us. Emotions are energy in motion. Newton taught us that an object in motion tends to stay in motion--unless acted upon by an unbalanced force. In this sense, the motion that wants to stay in motion is emotion, and the unbalanced force is the mind telling us not to feel it for any myriad of reasons.

As we are growing up and experiencing life, we each develop ways of handling situations that become habitual and restrict the flow of energy. It is so natural and familiar that after time we don't even realize what we're doing. We lose awareness of our responses to certain stimuli or situations. Anodea Judith teaches us in *Eastern Body Western Mind* that "Childhood traumas, cultural conditioning, limited belief systems, restrictive or exhausting habits, physical and emotional injuries, or even just lack of attention all contribute to chakra blockage."[2] A chakra is an energy center in the body that spins evenly when balanced. A chakra blockage is equivalent to an energy blockage. Energy blockages lead to a variety of different imbalances within the body. Therefore, energy healing activates the body's subtle energy systems to remove blocks, opening to the body's natural ability to heal itself.

"Energetic distortions can be found almost everywhere in our society and in ourselves, and are maintained through our lack of consciousness. If we can begin to understand the contortion of energy and do the hard work to transform it back to its natural flow, we have a good chance of effecting real change in ourselves and in the world we live in."[3] —Aimee Falchuk, MPH. M.Ed, CCE

Introduction

What exactly are the whispers of your heart? The whispers are those little love nudges you feel, sense or experience within your body. Sometimes it's a nagging sense that there's something more for you to do with your life. It might be the solution to a problem that just popped into your head. It can also be the nudge of inspiration to stay committed to what you are doing. The whispers could be any of these or none of these! Only you know how your heart whispers to you. One thing that is consistent with all whispers is exactly that--they are whispers. The nudges aren't noisy, mean, derogatory, judgmental, self-deprecating or filled with fear. We all hear plenty from that committee! This book is intended to guide you into the exploration of what makes you respond the way you do through what inspires you and everything in between.

Fall in Love is written to inspire curiosity, open to reflection, and step into an honest knowing of who you are. The book doesn't need to be read from cover to cover, but rather from a place of inspiration to read whatever random page you open to on any given day. There may be days where you take time to savor all aspects of the page, the quote, the musing, the reflection questions, and carry the mantra with you throughout your day. Some days may only be about catching the mantra. It may even be reading part of the page in the morning, being with it through the day, and returning to it in the evening. As you explore the reflection questions, remember to be gentle with yourself and give yourself the time and space you need. Create a comfy space, grab a cup of tea, and let curiosity guide you. Regardless of how you choose to use the book, trust that you are receiving whatever it is that you most need, even if some aspect irritates and chafes you and you don't open the book again for days or weeks or months.

Each chapter concludes with a page for you to be with your thoughts, jotting down what pops in your head, doodling as your mind wanders or whatever else it most needs to be. Simply allow. There are no rules--only the whispers of your heart.

This book was inspired by my own journey of personal and spiritual growth, which was catapulted into action after my divorce. I was faced with a whirlwind of unknowns, and my greatest resource was journaling. I felt too overwhelmed to attempt talking to anyone about how I was feeling, so I put pen to paper. I was able to release a lot of intense emotions and find calm. Every day for over a year, I dove in to explore. It was then that I received a mailing from a hospital that included classes for expectant mothers, geriatric care...and Reiki attunements. I would love to say that it has been smooth sailing from there, but that wouldn't be true. However, I can say that the exploration became richer and more fulfilling. It led me to completing training as an integrated energy and crystal healer and working with others to guide them in developing a relationship with their heart, mind, and body.

We all share a common journey, yet one that is uniquely our own. I can attest to the power of yes even when fear is chattering away noisily. My own work and curiosity have shifted my relationships, opened my awareness to triggers that needed healing, and inspired confidence and courage that I didn't even realize were so present within me. Even on the toughest of days, and there are plenty, I find this work to be rich and rewarding. I have met some incredible people--teachers really--along the way, and I am deeply grateful for their presence and support. We all need to find the space of gentleness and compassion for ourselves so we can expand our capacity to offer it to others.

Blessings on your journey to Fall in Love with the Whispers of Your Heart.

Table of Contents

The mind
noisy, grasping and busy

Seeking answers and searching for purpose
Feeling lost and alone ...
wondering, wandering and directionless

Groping in the darkness, waiting for a glimmer of light.
Then a whisper ... a whisper to come home.
Breathing
Scared
Unsure

The whisper returns, quietly nudging to be heard ...
Come home ... to your heart ... your sacred vault of truth
Be curious
Awaken
Love
Whispers of your heart

Prayer

For many, prayer is tied into the religious denomination in which we were raised. For some, this is a beautiful space of connection. For others, it can put up a wall of resistance. If you are one of the latter, fear not. You can change how you refer to prayer and move beyond the roadblock. You can call it communicating, offering gratitude, or even putting something out into the universe. Although prayers are used within religious institutions, prayer itself is not strictly contained within the institution. You can pray anytime, anywhere or anyhow. No rules. No restrictions. In all reality, you don't even need a clear concept to whom you are praying.

As Anne Lamott shares in her book *Help, Thanks, Wow*, "It [prayer] is communication from the heart to that which surpasses understanding. Let's say it is communication from one's heart to God."[4] Prayer helps bring comfort and opens your heart while connecting you to the greater good. Licensed Clinical Social Worker Alena Gerst reminds us that "prayers connect you to yourself."[5]

Take a breath,
be curious and explore
prayer in the whispers of your heart.

Prayer

A conversation opening to intimacy.

A plea in quiet desperation allowing our hearts to cry.

A blessing shining light upon us.

A connection spanning our lifetime.

A gift offering constant companionship.

Blessed be.

Prayer seems to be a matter of waiting in love, returning to love, trusting that love is the increasing stream of reality.

—Fr. Richard Rohr

Being raised in the Catholic faith and having attended a parochial K–8 school, prayer was taught to be very formal. To me, it felt like a required plea from a sinner to a savior. It felt rigid and disconnected. This is not to say that I don't have a connection to the prayers I have learned; it's that it felt transactional rather than relational. In order to build the relational aspect, it comes down to love. I have found a personal preference in referring to God as Divine Love. Once I shifted my perception around prayer and God, it started to feel more like a conversation, and I realized that nothing formal was required, no specific location or pious gesture. An openness to love is all that is needed.

Reflection Questions

What are your thoughts and beliefs around prayer?

How conscious is your choice around prayer?

What is that belief based on?

Mantra

When I choose to connect with prayer, I am supported.

Praying. It doesn't always have to be the blue iris, it could be weeds in a vacant lot, or a few small stones; just pay attention, then patch a few words together and don't try to make them elaborate, this isn't a contest but a doorway into thanks, and a silence in which another voice may speak.

—Mary Oliver

Praying is opening your heart and allowing everything to be seen—sadness, joy, pain, anger, needs, gratitude and everything in between. Be free of the "rules" or formality of prayer, and let it be genuine and raw. Whatever is in your heart is the most beautiful and sincere prayer you have to offer. Allow that to be enough. Give yourself over to the quiet of allowing a message in return. Be willing to receive your answer in any imaginable form, free of expectations and attachments. Listen. See. Breathe.

Reflection Questions
Take a deep breath and offer the words of your heart in prayer.

How did you react?

What did you notice?

Repeat the offering often, allowing yourself to get to know what's in your heart, too.

Mantra
**When I choose to open my heart in prayer,
I open myself to Love.**

Your sacred space is where you can find yourself again and again.

—Joseph Campbell

Although sacred space can be thought of as an actual physical location, think of it as being in your heart, listening to the quiet whispers and murmurs within. There is so much truth held in your heart: dreams, heartaches, memories, silence, serenity, love. And this is only the tip of the iceberg, for only you know what is in your heart and only you will understand the messages, which is why it is sacred. It's important to visit often because each day brings more and different opportunities, and the heart takes it all in and offers more insight. Connecting to your sacred space reminds you of your truth.

Reflection Questions

How often do you take time to connect to your heart?

What is behind the resistance of taking time?

What rules or beliefs do you hold around meditation or prayer?

What might you discover about yourself?

Mantra

**When I choose to listen to my heart,
my desires are revealed.**

In my deepest, darkest moments, what really got me through was a prayer. Sometimes my prayer was "Help me." Sometimes a prayer was "Thank you." What I've discovered is that intimate connection and communication with my creator will always get me through because I know my support, my help, is just a prayer away.

—Iyanla Vanzant

I can't even count the number of times that I have whispered, "Take this from me. It is too big." I have muttered this plea in moments of despair as well as moments of fatigue when things feel too overwhelming. Rarely do I specifically say what I need or want. All I know is that it opens me to receiving grace beyond my comprehension. I feel less alone and release the need to have all of the answers. Prayer is sharing what is on my heart, trusting that it is heard with love, and knowing that it is answered in love and that my fears don't stand a chance where love is deeply rooted.

Reflection Questions

What is your reaction to the concept of prayer?

What is your definition of prayer?

Where did that definition come from? Has it changed over the years?

What role, if any, does prayer play in your life?

Mantra

**When I choose to engage in prayer,
I live in love.**

Only in the quiet waters do things mirror themselves undistorted. Only in a quiet mind is adequate perception of the world.

—Hans Margolius

The mind can easily be filled with the noisy chatter of fear. Stories are created and elaborately developed that have no bearing of truth. Only when the mind is quiet are the whispers of the heart heard. The quiet mind hears the truth of the soul, and there are several ways to help tap into it. Journaling is one way to clear the clutter. Write what is on your mind, what you're feeling in your body and checking in with what is going on. After you clear the clutter, you are able to step into either meditation or prayer. While meditating, allow whatever comes up to do so. There are moments when meditating is only five minutes and other times when meditating is thirty minutes. There is no right or wrong when it comes to meditating. It's about taking deep breaths and allowing the mind to release its grip. Although prayer can carry a similar feeling to meditation, there is a slightly different intention. Prayer brings conversation and intentionally sharing what is on your mind and heart. The powerful connection with prayer and meditation is that one can easily lead into the other. Any way you look at it, the end result is the same: quiet your mind to gain clarity within and around you.

Reflection Questions

What do you do to create a quiet mind?

How often do you allow yourself to slow down enough to notice the chatter of the mind and to hear what it is saying?

How often do you allow yourself to ask, allow, and align?

Mantra

**When I choose to quiet my mind,
I hear truth.**

Whispers of your heart

_____

_____

_____

_____

_____

_____

_____

_____

Expectations

Expectations generally come attached to an outcome, which snowballs into attempting to control a situation and eventually leading to disappointment. Interestingly enough, you continue to set expectations and travel the familiar path over and over.

When I was auditioning for graduate school at Boston University, expectations were running rampant. I was letting ego steer the ship. "I was going to go to grad school for piano. Wow. That must mean I'm really talented. And to be on the East Coast, well, that definitely is high caliber." In reality, the confidence ego exuded was not the confidence my person exuded! I was notified that I was accepted into the graduate program...and I wasn't excited. Not at all. Paying attention to that sign would've been one choice, but I chose to ignore it and start classes in the fall. To say it went south in a hurry wouldn't be close to accurate. It proved to be an intense four months of working really hard and repeatedly being told that it wasn't good enough. During the winter break, I auditioned at UW-Milwaukee, got accepted and moved back to Wisconsin. Although the experience wasn't altogether better, I was free of expectation, choosing my growth experience over all else. I dug deep and accomplished my goal.

Christine Hassler, author of *Expectation Hangover,* shares, "When you have no expectations, you have no disappointments and you open yourself to the realm of infinite possibility, where happiness and abundance simply fall into your lap."[6]

Take a breath, be curious and explore what expectations are held in the whispers of your heart.

expectation …
attachment …
resistance …
disservice …
clinging …
grasping …
wanting …
unfulfilled …

breathe in …
breathe out …

Allow
Openness
Presence
Peace.

Expectation is the mother of all frustration.

—Antonio Banderas

Expectations take you out of the present moment. They place attachments on outcomes over which there is no control. You place expectations on people, vacations, job opportunities, and numerous things in between. Expectations are different than goals and dreams; they create assumptions. It's not uncommon to become complacent in behaviors when there are expectations involved. Responsibility gets shifted, and opportunities for growth are missed.

Reflection Questions
What was the most recent expectation you held?

Describe it as fully as possible.

Was that expectation met?

How did the situation unfold?

How did that result affect you?

How did you feel?

How did you react to the person(s) involved?

Mantra
**When I release expectation,
I am creative and flexible.**

It's your own expectations that hurt you. Not the world you live in. Whatever happens in the world is real. What you think should happen is unreal. So people are hurt by their expectations. You know, you're not disappointed by the world, you are disappointed by your own projections.

—Jacque Fresco

Your vision can easily become clouded with expectation, wrapped in fear. You want things to go a certain way or for people to react in a specific way. For example, you share something with your spouse and hold an expectation for their response. This can also happen when you share a new idea with friends or family members. Anything other than the response you are seeking and craving can derail you. In a sense, what you really want is acceptance and affirmation. If someone reacts the way you expect them to, you receive the affirmation that you don't offer to yourself. It's one thing to set a goal to work toward; it's another thing to expect that everything will always go as you want it to. The outer affirmations and acceptance are always a gift, but it is important to learn to affirm and accept your own self as unconditionally as possible.

Reflection Questions

Describe an experience that did not turn out as you expected.

What were you looking for?

How did that experience affect you?

What can you gain from this awareness?

Mantra

**When I choose to accept myself,
I allow life to unfold for me.**

We are all addicted to our own habitual way of doing anything, our own defenses, and most especially our patterned way of thinking, or how we process our reality. By definition, you can never see or handle what you are addicted to. You cannot heal what you do not first acknowledge.

—Fr. Richard Rohr

How often have you heard yourself say, "It's just who I am," or "I have always done that"? The phrases are excuses, ways of dodging responsibility and resisting change. Perhaps it's when you find yourself doing things you don't want to because people expect that you will jump in and take care of it. And you do. Either pattern becomes so familiar that you may not even realize that you are the one choosing the response and repeatedly creating the habit. The patterns become so ingrained that you don't consider the repercussions on your own self. When you awaken to the reality of the habit, the thought of changing it can be overwhelming. The fear of rejection or disappointing someone else becomes so strong that it can be challenging to break the pattern. Release the expectation and make yourself responsible for your "stuff" only. Others will find their way, move through their emotions, and move on.

Reflection Questions

What is one thing you find yourself continually doing only because somebody else expects you to?

Why do you keep doing it?

What would it take to help you choose you instead of someone else?

Mantra

**When I choose to act in ways that honor me,
I release resentment.**

Unhappiness is best defined as the difference between our talents and our expectations.

—Edward de Bono

Expectations fill your mind with anything but what is in front of you. It is a challenging reality that you spend your time attempting to fix what is wrong with you rather than embracing the talents you already possess. Being aware of your talents and utilizing them to the best of your ability in any given moment releases attachment to expectation, allowing for the deep inner connection to feed you. There is an assumed expectation that happiness is achieved by an outside experience. When you step into your talents and embrace them for your own benefit and not for an expected response from someone else, you experience gratification that no other person could give you.

Reflection Questions

What expectation(s) do you find yourself being reminded of regularly?

What is the motivator behind that?

How do you feel when the sense of expectation is upon you?

When do you feel happiest?

Mantra

**When I choose to release expectations,
I am free to experience happiness.**

The universe has no restrictions. You place restrictions on the universe with your expectations.

—Deepak Chopra

This can be a tough concept to accept. It can be easier to place blame on the external challenges that continually come your way instead of seeing how your mindset and choices contribute to the creation of the situation. It's important to pay attention to what thoughts run through your head regarding life and how it has unfolded, especially how you respond to struggles. You have to contribute to your journey without placing expectations on the outcomes. The ability to stay open and present to the unfolding allows there to be freedom from expectations. If you expect things to go a certain way, the mind can become restricted and inflexible when the end result is different. Or if you expect a certain outcome, you may miss an opportunity right before you. Stay open to the influence and support of the universe and things will flow differently. See your life experiences as messengers and be curious.

Reflection Questions

What is your common course of action when you get an idea?

What is your level of willingness to take action if everything isn't laid out and definitive?

How has your belief of universal support influenced your life?

Mantra

**When I choose to be open and receptive,
I experience abundance.**

Whispers of your heart

_____

_____

_____

_____

_____

_____

_____

_____

Being Heard

Being heard helps fulfill the basic human need of connection, which starts by engaging and responding. When you can listen without planning a response, you are able to open to what is actually being said. When the defenses rise or you get distracted by planning the retort, you often miss the point of what is being said.

"We would not, hopefully, go up to another person's work of art and scribble all over it, or black it out with dark paint. However, when we do not acknowledge what another is saying, thinking or feeling, the effect is the same."[7]

—Gwen Randall-Young, psychologist

There are times when being heard can be a real head-scratcher. I've had experiences where I have been asked my opinion for either A or B; I say B and the immediate action is A. Then why even bother to ask? Was the question for appearances only?

On the flip side of that, it is important to be aware of how you are speaking because that can influence whether or not there is a capacity to be heard. For example, if you approach someone when you are in a swirling tizzy, are speaking fast and barely breathing, you may not be heard because your overwhelm just overwhelmed the person to whom you are talking. It boils down to awareness.

Take a breath, be curious and open to hearing
the whispers of your heart.

Teach me to listen to the wisdom of my feet:

-modeling strength and connection
-supporting me on Mother Earth
-telling tales of journeys experienced

Teach me to listen to the wisdom of my hands:

-hearing unspoken words through touching another
-laboring through life, creating in every moment
-caressing with tenderness and love

Teach me to listen to the wisdom of my intuition:

-trusting my inner knowing
-remembering my divine connection
-believing in all I sense
-showering light in the darkness

Teach me to listen to the wisdom of my heart:

-holding dreams waiting to be fulfilled
-embracing my worthiness
-informing my mind
-guiding my life
-singing songs still needing to be sung

Teach me to listen to the wisdom of love.

People start to heal the moment they feel heard.

—Cheryl Richardson

There is deep significance in the value of being heard. Oftentimes, what you want to be heard takes great courage and vulnerability to share in the first place. When what is shared is met with no response, a dismissive response, or a defensive reaction, there is an additional aspect to be healed on top of the fear of repeating the process all over. However, if what is shared is met with compassion and understanding, the first layer of guardedness can melt away and soften what remains underneath. Everybody has stories and events that have influenced who they are today. When you openly welcome receiving somebody else's story, you also receive the gift of healing, knowing that you are not alone.

Reflection Questions

What lies heavy on your heart that you need to have heard?

Who would you feel safe and comfortable with sharing the information?

When in your life have you offered the gift of healing through hearing someone's story?

Mantra

**When I am heard,
my heart softens.**

Being safe is about being seen and heard and allowed to be who you are and to speak your truth.

—Rachel Naomi Remen

This quote carries truth around emotional safety. The general tendency to be safe seems to lead people to the idea of physical safety. Although that is very real, emotional safety is a completely different concept and is often overlooked. Emotional safety creates a sacred space of vulnerability, offering acceptance for feeling what you feel. Emotional safety softens the fear of being seen and heard, just as it invites the you within to be alive. Feeling emotionally safe brings the trust that you will be heard and accepted.

Reflection Questions

What does "emotional safety" mean to you?

What do you need in order to feel emotionally safe?

In what ways do you offer or provide emotional safety for others?

How do you offer emotional safety to yourself?

Mantra

When I choose to trust in emotional safety, I am seen in my truth.

Communication is not saying something; communication is being heard.

—Frances Hesselbein

Communication is an exchange of ideas with openness and mutual presence. It doesn't need to be deep and pensive. True communication is a sign of respect. It is far too common for people to talk without being acknowledged or given the respect of stopping whatever activity is at hand and tuning in. It also seems that this is quite prevalent at home more than anywhere else. It's as though the "safety" of home invites a disengagement from being present. Engage. Connect. Communicate.

Reflection Questions

How does it feel when you say something and it is followed by silence?

What kind of communicator are you?

How often do you engage and really listen as part of communication?

Mantra

When I choose to be present with another in communication, I honor myself and the person I am with.

Everyone wants to be seen. Everyone wants to be heard.
Everyone wants to be recognized as the person that they are and
not a stereotype or an image.

—Loretta Lynch

There are times when the desire to be seen and heard is met head-on with your fear of being seen and heard. This can create confusion and falsely placed blame. When there is a passion to be seen for who you are, are you taking the steps necessary to allow that to happen, or are you hiding in the shadows? And if the moment passes, are you taking responsibility for not stepping into the opportunity, or are you blaming someone else for not offering it to you? If there is a situation where you feel you are not being heard, are you speaking up, clearly articulating what you mean or need, or are you blaming another for not hearing what you meant? Being heard does require a personal mental sense of clarity, knowing specifically what it is that you need or want. Speaking vaguely or using phrases that don't make sense to the other person doesn't help accomplish your need. Step into the desire to be seen and heard and known for who you are. Empower yourself. You deserve it.

Reflection Questions
How often do you allow yourself to be seen in the fullness of you and your talents?

How would you describe your ability to clearly state what you mean or need?

How do you respond in large group situations?

Do you try to blend in or be you?

Mantra

**When I choose to step into being seen and heard,
I honor myself.**

Being heard is so close to being loved that for the average person they are almost indistinguishable.

—David Augsburger

The notion of being heard is often satirized in comic strips, sitcoms, or comedic movies, typically with the wife wanting to know if her husband heard her. It's easy to laugh at because it is so relatable. In reality, it's not so funny because, on the surface, it often sends a message of disrespect. There are often a multitude of reasons why people tune each other out: · "You nag too much." · "I heard you the first time." · "I'm afraid of making you mad." · "Why does it matter if I answer you because you'll do whatever you want anyway/you won't believe me?" It often becomes an endless battle of which came first, the chicken or the egg. Peel away the layers, and it is about being loved—from either side.

Reflection Questions

What is your experience around being heard?

How important is it to you?

How attentive are you to others when they speak?

Are you consistent with every person, or do you listen based on how well you like them?

Describe a time when you felt heard.

Who were you with?

What were you sharing with them?

How did the other person respond?

Mantra

When I choose to listen with an open heart, I create connection with another person.

Whispers of your heart

_____

_____

_____

_____

_____

_____

_____

_____

Judgment

Judgment is a distorted concept. Fear of being judged by others is quite common, yet you tend to judge your own self more than anybody else does. The self-judgment then leads to avalanche-building fear stories. As mind/body psychotherapist Dr. Ronald Alexander states, "The object is to stop assigning meaning to these self-judgments because once you start to give them weight, they begin to weigh you down. Elaborating on these judgments will cause you to feel constricted by your unwholesome thought processes."[8]

The feared result of judgment is being rejected or unlovable. If you can deepen your own sense of self-love and self-acceptance, you will be more likely to offer acceptance to others. It will open you to the reality of what you are experiencing instead of the story being created. Guy Finley, spiritual teacher and self-help author, shares, "When we impose a negative view on things and people based on the past conditioning we bring to the moment, we can't experience life directly or see the good it may be offering."[9]

Take a breath, be curious and listen to
the whispers of your heart...
free of judgment.

incessant berating that clamors in the mind, creating pressure to do more ...

to be more ...

telling stories of belittlement ...

ineptitude ...

reliving moments to evaluate responses and reactions ...

craving quiet ...

stillness ...

acceptance ...

Love.

When you judge another, you do not define them, you define yourself.

—Wayne Dyer

Judging others often reflects an unhealed wound within you. It is like holding up a mirror to see what you are unwilling or unable to see in yourself. The more intense the judgment of others, the closer the wound is to the surface, just waiting to be released. Judgment can also be a mask for your own personal insecurity. Bringing attention to another through judgment takes the attention off of you, seemingly freeing you of responsibility and ownership.

Reflection Questions
When was the last time you passed judgment on someone?

What did you say?

What was your intent when passing judgment?

How does this reflect back on you?

Mantra
**When I choose to release judgment,
I accept others as well as myself.**

We can never judge the lives of others because each person knows only their own pain and renunciation. It's one thing to feel that you are on the right path, but it's another to think that yours is the only path.

—Paulo Coelho

Generally speaking, you judge what is unfamiliar. To add to it, there is a tendency to judge the person and not the actions or words. You can cultivate acceptance when you foster curiosity. You shape your life or choices based on the experiences you have had. There is no good or bad, right or wrong. It simply is. The difference in experiences can create a rich diversity of connection—if you allow for it.

Reflection Questions
What was the last thing you judged another person about?

What does that judgment reflect about you?

What can you gain from this awareness?

Mantra
When I choose to accept the differences of those around me, I accept myself.

*You, therefore, have no excuse, you who pass judgment on
someone else, for at whatever point you judge another, you are
condemning yourself, because you who pass judgment do the
same things.*

—Romans 2:1 (NIV)

When judgment of another person starts infiltrating your mind,
know that you are struggling with something that has yet to come
to your complete awareness. It's ego's way of distracting you from
your own self and putting attention—or blame—on someone else.
This is the time for you to be curious and understand what is going
on: What are you ignoring? What is bringing up these judgments?
Are you guilty of doing the very thing that you are judging? For
example, if you're desiring more gratitude for the things you do,
are you offering gratitude to others for what they do? It is an
interesting path: following the judgment, being curious, and gaining
understanding.

Reflection Questions

What is the most recent judgment you passed on another person
(in your head or aloud)?

Do you believe it to be true?

What did it stem from?

What nugget did you learn about yourself?

Mantra

**When I choose to disengage from judgment,
I am free to love.**

The more one judges, the less one loves.

—Honoré de Balzac

Love involves acceptance, which is the opposite of judgment. Judgment involves fear, like fear of exposure. If you can divert attention away from you so nobody can see your flaws, you erroneously feel safe. Have you ever argued with someone and you throw judgments or insults at them? It's an effort to mask your own self-judgment and pain by dumping all responsibility onto them. It allows you to avoid seeing your own personal contribution to the situation along with avoiding the pain within. Notice what comes up when you are at odds with another person. It will help you see what unhealed wound is being triggered and open the door to healing. It's powerful to choose love for you and for others.

Reflection Questions

What part of you could use more love and acceptance?

How might this shift the responsibility away from the judgment of others?

When do you notice yourself judging others most often?

Mantra

**When I choose to love myself,
I love others with ease.**

Placing the blame or judgment on someone else leaves you powerless to change your experience; taking responsibility for your beliefs and judgments gives you the power to change them.

—Byron Katie

Placing blame helps avoid feeling the uncomfortable feelings that lie just beneath the surface. It projects feelings of unworthiness onto another person instead of acknowledging the feelings of unworthiness within. Placing blame also casts a cloak of shame onto the other person rather than feeling the guilt of making a choice that didn't go as intended or a reaction that didn't fit the situation. There is a deep level of honesty and vulnerability involved when taking responsibility for your own beliefs and judgments. It fosters an understanding of what you bring to the table and offers the insight to change. Every person has a story within. Be willing to read between the lines and understand the meaning behind your judgment of others.

Reflection Questions

Describe a recent time when you placed blame or judged another person?

Why did you do it?

What were you experiencing in that moment?

What other choices could you have made?

Mantra

When I choose to take responsibility for my words and actions, I create peace.

Whispers of your heart

_____

_____

_____

_____

_____

_____

_____

_____

Connection

Acceptance, vulnerability, and trust are all interwoven within connection. The combination creates a safe space where freedom to be you exists. Holistic psychologist and PhD Ellie Cobb affirms, "Fear can get in the way of creating connection. When we experience fear, our brain is in survival mode, not connective mode. Before we can connect, our brain needs to feel safe."[10]

In the space of vulnerability, trust, and acceptance, the body experiences freedom and fluidity. The fight or flight response within the body is deactivated, and the mind experiences peace. This place of physical freedom and presence support connection in a pure, unaltered way. As a best-selling author, Shannon Kaiser states, "If you want to increase your connection with a loved one, start by giving them permission to be themselves. The more we can be true to ourselves, the easier it is to flourish in relationships."[11]

**Take a breath, be curious and connect
with the whispers of your heart.**

Love me.

Exactly as I am.

Love the parts of me that make sense.

Love the parts of me that don't.

Love the parts of me that scare you because of how they make you feel inside.

Love the parts of me that inspire and intrigue you

Love the parts of me that intimidate.

Love the parts of me that challenge you to grow.

Love my successes.

Love my mistakes.

Love my quirks.

Love my humor.

Love my intelligence.

Love my ignorance.

Love my OCD qualities.

Love my that'll-do qualities.

Love the me who remembers.

Love the me who forgets.

Love the me who is gentle and compassionate.

Love the me who is snarky.

Love the me who is patient.

Love the me who is frustrated.

Love and accept me for who I am.

All of me.

*The need for connection and community is
primal, as fundamental as the need for air, water, and food.*

—Dean Ornish

When you long for connection with others, you may or may not
identify it as such or be able to put it into words. Maybe you
find yourself mindlessly going through your day and never really
engaging with anyone. There is a hollow, empty feeling of being
solitary, even if you live with other people. Sometimes the lack
of connection with others is rooted in a need to check in with
yourself. Have you numbed yourself from feeling, being inspired
or engaging with your own needs? When you are feeling connected
to yourself, it feels easier to connect with others and the feeling of
isolation subsides.

Reflection Questions

How would you describe your connection with your own Self?

Reflect on your dreams, fears, passions, strengths, or areas of
growth as starting points.

Describe your comfort and connection with other people.

Whom do you feel most connected to?

What inspires the connection?

Mantra

**When I choose to foster connection,
I am supported.**

So, the opposite of addiction is not sobriety. It is human connection.

—Johann Hari

Addictions come in many forms: shopping, eating, drugs, alcohol, busy-ness, gaming, smoking, gambling, hoarding, and many more. It's not uncommon for the behavior to start as a way to avoid emotions or to fill an unnamable "void" within. As a general cultural collective, uncomfortable emotions are ignored as much as possible. If you're not feeling happy, elated, joyful, or something of that nature, the preference is to numb or ignore it. You attempt to find ways to get around it instead of reaching out to someone and getting your concerns off your chest. Knowing there is someone in your corner in a gentle, compassionate way invites you to break the cycle. There is an opportunity to receive love and support for who you are at this moment, knowing there is someone willing to walk with you on your journey to deeper connection and balance.

Reflection Questions
What is your habitual go-to when you feel overwhelmed?

When did this habit start?

Was it prompted by an event in your life?

Or maybe a learned response?

What do you most need in those moments of overwhelm?

Mantra
When I choose to be mindful of my habits, I am grounded and present in the moment.

I define connection as the energy that exists between people when they feel seen, heard, and valued; when they can give and receive without judgment; and then they derive sustenance and strength from the relationship.

—Brené Brown

It is easy to put the responsibility on someone else when it comes to connection; to blame someone else for their lack of effort in a relationship. It is essential to take an honest look at yourself and take note of what is being contributed. You can't wait for a connection to happen without a willingness to encourage it and be open to it. You have to be willing to be seen and heard in order to feel seen and heard.

Reflection Questions
How do you step into the vulnerability of being seen and heard?

In what ways do you cultivate a relationship of a judgment-free zone?

How do you offer yourself the opportunity to be seen and heard, valuing yourself without the clamor of judgment?

Mantra
**When I choose to value myself,
I am open to connection with others.**

Human connections are deeply nurtured in the field of shared story.

—Jean Houston

Many examples support this quote, but the first one that popped into my head is the grief of losing a beloved pet. Although we had family pets growing up and I felt sad when they passed, it was very different losing my companion of almost fifteen years, Wolfgang. Since many knew of his passing, I received a lot of support. On top of it, though, was the realization of how many other people came to me with the aging struggles of their pets. I became a source of empathy and support for people, some of whom I only had casual passing conversations with, simply because of a shared story. Some have since lost their pets, and there is a connection in sharing the grief journey with them, being very vulnerable about the roller coaster of emotions for an animal. Animal lovers know that it is far more than "just" an animal, but sometimes the rational mind prevents allowing the grief to exist as fully as it needs to be felt. When there is connection with another person or people, it becomes safe to feel and be present with the experience.

Reflection Questions

Recall a time where an experience of yours created a shared-story connection with another person.

What was the impact of that on you?

How has that shifted your willingness to be more present with other experiences in your life?

How might that experience influence your interaction with others?

Mantra

When I choose to share my experiences, I am supported.

Deep human connection is ... the purpose and the result of a meaningful life—and it will inspire the most amazing acts of love, generosity, and humanity.

—Melinda Gates

Human connection feeds the sense of community, fostering a natural desire to be part of the whole. You see this often in times of crisis or tragedy when entire communities pull together to recover and regroup. How can you foster this connection in the everyday? Even within your closer-knit circles, you might find yourself not fully allowing the deep connection to be there. Maybe it is within a family unit where you don't feel like you fit in, or you don't understand why people make the choices they make. Opening your hearts to connection makes room for acceptance, allowing each person to be who they are without their actions or words making the determination for them.

Reflection Questions

Think of your family unit.

What keeps you from making room for a deep connection with them?

How can you soften around that?

What actions or words come from you that deflect others' willingness to connect with you?

What needs to shift in your perception to make you more approachable?

Mantra

When I choose to be seen for who I am,
I open myself to connection with others.

Whispers of your heart

Anger

Anger tends to be perceived as an ugly emotion and treated as taboo. However, if you use it instead of spew it, you can understand what is behind it. Sex and relationship editor at MindBodyGreen, Kelly Gonsalves states, "Anger is perhaps the most maligned and misunderstood emotion of all; we're exceedingly anxious to shut it down when we feel it, to fear or be repulsed by others who display it and to try to avoid it at all costs. But like with any other emotion, not being able to understand or process our anger can lead to a lot of psychological distress."[12]

It is also helpful to understand your unique physical response to anger. When you are aware of what manifests in your body when you are experiencing anger, you can move through the anger before it has the opportunity to get bottled up and spit out later.

Take a breath, be curious and explore
what the whispers of your heart reveal about anger.

Anger

volatile ... explosive ... unpredictable ...

What is behind your fury?
Why do you manipulate me?

spewing ... spitting ... seething ...

What are you afraid of?
What feeds your fire?

aggressive ... bombastic ... debilitating ...

Let me see you.
Let me understand.

incessant ... controlling ... piercing ...

I am not afraid of you.
Let me help you find peace.

Where there is anger, there is always pain underneath.

—Eckhart Tolle

Anger can be an unshakeable shield to pain if you allow it to be so. It is often easier to be angry than to lean into it and feel the pain beneath it. It really isn't easier at all, but it mistakenly feels safer. A common thought is that the pain is too much to handle or appears as a weakness; therefore, no one is going to see the pain or the vulnerability of experiencing pain. Since anger is an emotion that generally has a negative connotation, it can be challenging to lean in and discover the story underneath. When you experience resistance around an emotion such as anger, explore ways that might encourage you, such as using the acronym for the word: **A**nother **N**ew **G**rowth **E**xperience **R**evealed. This can soften the resistance to anger and bring in curiosity, which then reveals the pain and allows the healing to happen.

Reflection Questions

Describe the last time you felt angry.

What triggered the anger?

If you have not already done so, explore what was behind the anger.

Mantra

When I choose to explore my feelings of anger, I offer healing to myself.

Explain your anger, instead of expressing it, and you will find solutions instead of arguments.

—Ritu Ghatourey

Anger can be a scary dance partner; you're never quite sure what the next step is going to be. This alone is often enough to make people steer clear of any aspect of anger. Getting to know anger as a dance partner reveals the steps to a fluid, enjoyable dance of life. Explaining your anger may need to be a solitary experience first until there is more ease and familiarity in the process. Many would rather not experience anger at all, much less become chummy with it. However, building a relationship with the anger that comes up eventually leads to less anger overall. Being curious about the anger and what is behind it leads to understanding and growth, not to mention avoiding hurt feelings and arguments.

Reflection Questions

Describe the last time someone or something brought up feelings of anger.

What were you afraid of?

How was that situation resolved?

What is your reaction when you experience someone else's anger directed toward you?

Mantra

**When I choose to explain anger,
I experience peace.**

Speak when you are angry and you will make the best speech you will ever regret.

—Ambrose Bierce

Anger is a hot emotion that can create damage when it is not understood. Anger often hides fear with a painful experience behind it. Since my childhood included witnessing hot tempers, my tendency is to back away from anger in all forms. When I witness anger, I tend to become paralyzed in both thought and action. When I feel anger, my mind starts racing, my stomach starts churning, and I notice heat rising within. That's when I take a deep breath and bring my awareness down to my feet. Oftentimes, this helps me regain perspective and slow down the racing thoughts in my head. From there, I step into the curiosity of what is behind the anger and peel back the layers. I am often able to get to the root of it and make a calm decision as to what, if anything, needs to be done. It's acceptable to feel anger. It's not acceptable to act out in anger. Big difference.

Reflection Questions

How does your body respond to anger, either yours or someone else's?

What is your overall reaction to anger, yours and someone else's?

What, if anything, triggers feelings of anger?

Mantra

When I choose to explore anger, I understand more about myself.

A man is about as big as the things that make him angry.

—Winston Churchill

Anger often masks fear. If you shift the quote to read, "A man is about as big as the things he fears," a new perspective is gained. Anger becomes less repulsive if you allow the concept of fear into the picture. When you feel anger rising, you can invite yourself to be curious about what you are afraid of in that moment. If you are witnessing someone else's anger, the same idea can be applied. In either situation, knowing that fear is lurking behind the anger opens a space of compassion and lessens the defensiveness. The only way to soften anger is to understand the fear underneath it and use it wisely to inform in order to transform. The more the fear is ignored, the bigger and more reprehensible the anger. Instead of acting out in a swirl of fear and anger, open yourself to gentleness, and lead from the heart.

Reflection Questions

What is something that stirs up the fiery emotion of anger?

What is the fear that is hiding behind that?

How can you use that to weaken the anger trigger?

Mantra

When I choose to understand my feelings of anger, I am compassionate.

It is impossible for you to be angry and laugh at the same time. Anger and laughter are mutually exclusive and you have the power to choose either.

—Wayne Dyer

You choose anger or laughter. You do. Nobody else makes the choice for you. You get to choose. I get to choose. Nobody can make you angry. Nobody can make you laugh. It's a choice, one you allow to happen. Repeatedly. There may be people in your life who bring out the laughter easily, but it is still your choice how to respond to them. There may also be people in your life who don't laugh much at all, but that doesn't mean you don't get to choose laughter. And your laughter may very well make the other respond in anger, but that's their choice. The brilliant thing about laughter is that even if you start off feeling angry, attempt laughing, and stick with it long enough, it turns into genuine laughter. My sister and I proved this theory to be true late one night when we were in our late teens and sharing a room again at home. I would venture a guess that it was my sister who started it (since I don't remember that detail), suggesting that we see how many different ways we can "fake" laugh. It was quite hysterical and eventually led to both of us laughing for real. I remember my dad saying he wanted to record us, but he thought we would stop by the time he got his recorder set up. He had plenty of time! So, remember: you have the choice—laughter or anger. Make it a worthwhile choice.

Reflection Questions

Recall a time when you felt angry. How could that have been handled with laughter?

Which is the more automatic, default response for you: laughter or anger?

How often do you engage in laughter?

Mantra

**When I choose laughter,
I am open to the flow of life.**

Whispers of your heart

_____

_____

_____

_____

_____

_____

_____

_____

Joy

The Merriam-Webster Dictionary defines joy as "the emotion evoked by well-being, success, or good fortune or by the prospect of possessing what one desires." This can lead to believing that joy is something that occurs from an outside influence. I, personally, align more with Dr. Cheryl A. MacDonald who states, "Joy is a state of mind, a combination of emotions. Joy contains elements of contentment, confidence, and hope. Joy is an inner conscious belief."[13] Joy is the deep connection to your own self; a place that brings calm in the storms of life. It is noticing what you're feeling inside and compassionately accepting it as your experience in this moment, not panicking or stressing out because of the feelings.

Take a breath, be curious and discover
joy in the whispers of your heart.

Divine Spirit,

Guide my sadness to know Your joy.

Guide my pain to know Your healing.

Guide my anger to know Your grace.

Guide my shame to know Your mercy.

Guide my uncertainty to know Your wisdom.

Guide my fear to know Your love.

Guide my life to be aligned with You.

Joy is prayer. Joy is strength. Joy is love. Joy is a net of love by which you can catch souls.

—Mother Teresa

Not only is joy a sense of pleasure or happiness, but joy is also connection to Self. When you are connected within, everything flows from the place of inner peace and joy. Knowing what you are feeling within guides the prayer, feeds the strength, and opens to love. The net of love is only as big as the connection to joy. The more you know the whispers of your heart, the more your joy will encourage others.

Reflection Questions
When was the last time you listened to the whispers of your heart?

What do you most need at this moment?

What can you do to honor that need?

How does it feel to know what you need?

Mantra
**When I choose to listen to my heart,
I experience joy.**

Happiness arrives not in the absence of problems, but in the absence of rules about when you can feel it.

—The Universe (a.k.a. Mike Dooley)

There are cultural and societal norms that define what happiness is and when you can feel it. Happiness feels more accessible when you accept that life involves struggles and challenges to continually help you grow, learn, and love more. When you make room for life, you make room for happiness. Happiness isn't about pretending that everything in life is easy and fluid. Happiness is a space of peace and presence. Being present with all that life has to offer, easy or challenging, urges you to be grateful that you are here experiencing it.

Reflection Questions
How do you describe happiness?

When was the most recent time you can recall feeling happy? Describe it.

What prevents you from feeling happy?

Mantra
When I choose to be present and experience life as it is, I create space for happiness.

When you do things from your soul, you feel a river moving in you, a joy.

—Rumi

I associate connection and joy with the "flow" state—being deeply immersed in what is feeding my soul at that moment and losing track of time. I always walk away from those experiences feeling deeply satisfied and content, wishing that the feeling didn't have to end. Even in the event that I don't have unlimited time, soul connection still happens, and everything flows smoothly. When things don't feel like they are flowing smoothly, slow down and pay attention. Is it the actual event, the person, or the way you are going about completing the task? This understanding will offer clarity around connecting to the joy within.

Reflection Questions

What activity opens you to the "flow" state?

How would you describe what it feels like to be in the flow state?

How can you open to that place of connection in your daily activities?

Mantra

When I choose to open to the flow within, I experience ease.

Joy is not in things; it is in us.

—Richard Wagner

It is common to witness people buying more, doing more, or traveling more to find happiness. You can seek outside of you, but you won't find true joy and happiness. It is within you. There is an element of choice involved, too. You can choose to have a grateful heart or be upset that you don't have as much as your coworker. You can choose to take part in activities that you enjoy or bemoan never doing anything fun. You can choose to create a life you want to live or blame the powers that be for not giving it to you. The examples could continue yet the message remains the same: you choose. There is extreme joy in the empowerment of choice—and it all lies within you.

Reflection Questions
What do you expect will bring you joy?

What keeps you from choosing joy?

How do you feel when you see others experiencing happiness?

Mantra
**When I choose joy,
I find peace.**

Joy is the holy fire that keeps our purpose warm and our intelligence aglow.

—Helen Keller

Joy, connection to Self, is a sacred fire within. On the days when it feels like the world is upside down and inside out, joy is a source of inspiration. Taking a moment to connect within reminds you of the why. Why am I doing this? Why is this important to me? Joy ignites the passion within and brings about the courage to carry on. Joy reminds you to be grateful for all that you have and to keep things in perspective. Joy reminds you that all things are temporary, be it happy or sad, and to savor every moment.

Reflection Questions
How do you define joy?

How often do you experience a sense of joy?

What interferes with joy being more present in your life?

Mantra
**When I choose to experience joy,
I experience fullness in each moment.**

Whispers of your heart

Sadness

Sadness is a time when you long for comfort yet make an attempt to be happy because there is no reason to be sad, or so your mind tries to tell you. The Director of Greater Good Science Center at Berkeley University, Dacher Keltner, supports leaning into sadness. He says, "In our culture, we're tough on sadness, but it's a powerful trigger for seeking comfort and bonding."[14] When you are accepted in your sadness, a deeper connection is made. However, seeing others in their sadness can make people feel uncomfortable and want to fix the situation. A familiar strain involves telling you that you shouldn't feel that way. Another constant reminder within our culture that can deter you from leaning into sadness is about having a positive attitude. Joseph P. Forgas, Ph.D. and professor of psychology, states, "Findings from my own research suggest that sadness can help people improve attention to external details, reduce judgmental bias, increase perseverance, and promote generosity. All of these findings build a case that sadness has some adaptive functions, and so should be accepted as an important component of our emotional repertoire."[15]

Take a breath, be curious and discover
more about sadness in the whispers of your heart.

Sadness...

the vacancy

the despair

the void

*the blanket over your heart seemingly to bring comfort
that suffocates instead*

*hearing your favorite song on the radio but unable
to sing along*

emotional drain leaving you hollow and spent

*wanting to engage in conversation, but your mind is
a blank canvas without color or inspiration*

*seeing the beauty around you and unable to allow it
to touch your heart.*

Lean in, dear one, and be gentle.

Sadness has depth that opens to joy.

Tears are words that need to be written.

—Paulo Coelho

Tears need permission to be shed. They are the body's natural reset button. Sometimes tears just need to fall because they are right under the surface and need to be released, free of any reason why. Tears are often easier to cry than words are spoken. Tears contain stories of the heart waiting to be told.

Reflection Questions
When was the last time you shed tears?

How did you feel afterward?

What is your typical response when you feel tears coming?

What is your response when you see others crying?

Mantra
**When I choose to allow myself to cry,
I give my body the opportunity to reset.**

Every human walks around with a certain kind of sadness. They may not wear it on their sleeves, but it's there if you look deep.

—Taraji P. Henson

This quote is helpful on two levels. First of all, it loosens the grip on the need to always be happy. It gives permission to feel how you feel without thinking that everyone else is always happy or has such a great or easy life. It's not to say that there aren't moments of ease and grace, but everyone carries a story within their heart that may contain feelings of sadness. The other aspect holds the reminder that you are called to treat others with gentleness and compassion because you don't know their story and you don't know how close it is to the surface. Every day offers a different emotional disposition and it is important to remember that it applies to everyone, not just you. We are all touched by events in our lives, and regardless of how accepting each individual is around this idea, we all have permission to feel and be where we are. We also don't have to make the situation different for anyone, either. We're really all the same, simply making different choices.

Reflection Questions
What sadness are you carrying today?

What might help bring peace or resolution?

Mantra
When I choose to know my sadness, I grow in love.

Grief can have a quality of profound healing because we are forced to a depth of feeling that is usually below the threshold of awareness.

—Stephen Levine

Anyone who has experienced the loss of a loved one understands grief. The deeper level of experiencing the healing from grief involves leaning into it when it shows up again and again. The question becomes whether you allow yourself to feel the grief that is masked by anger, feeling overwhelmed, irritability, or any other disguise. This is the depth of grief that lies below the threshold of awareness. This is also the depth of grief that happens weeks, months or even years after the event. There is no time frame for grief. The invitation is to lean into the healing that grief offers, knowing that the more deeply you love, the more deeply you grieve.

Reflection Questions
Describe a time when you experienced a loss that included grief. How did you handle that moment?

How has the grief reappeared since that event?

What tools are available to you to lean into the grief and allow for continued healing?

Mantra
**When I choose to feel grief,
I open myself to loving deeply.**

Even a happy life cannot be without a measure of darkness, and the word happy would lose its meaning if it were not balanced by sadness.

—Carl Jung

There needs to be balance in the opposites, or you could easily start to take things for granted. You wouldn't know light without darkness, connection without isolation, love without fear, compassion without rejection, or joy without sadness. Avoid pushing away the uncomfortable one from a place of resistance. Lean in and feel the discomfort because that is how the impermanence of the discomfort finds release. The opposites invite you to feel life as fully as possible and embrace what is offered. The deeper you feel sadness, the greater the connection when it releases and reveals happiness.

Reflection Questions

What do you use as a barometer for a happy life?

What aspct of your life do you feel is lacking?

How can you bring balance to that area?

Mantra

When I choose to embrace opposites, I am in balance.

There is a sacredness in tears. They are not the mark of weakness, but of power. They speak more eloquently than ten thousand tongues. They are the messengers of overwhelming grief, of deep contrition, and of unspeakable love.

—Washington Irving

Tears can speak all of the words that your heart cannot utter. There was a stretch of time in my life when I was experiencing one devastating blow after another: divorce, a flooded basement that took everything that was stored there, a near fire from electrical damage after the flood, lack of money to tend to all that needed to be repaired, and the events continued. During that time, I didn't cry. Not once. My aunt passed away unexpectedly, and I didn't cry. Then a few years later, my uncle passed away unexpectedly, and I didn't cry, and these were relatives who were very present in my life. For almost five years, I couldn't cry. Then one day, during a commercial (I'm almost positive it was for Folger's Coffee), a single tear streaked down my cheek. I was elated! I was finding my way back to feeling and accepting the depth of what life had to offer. Now it takes very little for the tears to come, be it sadness, happiness, love—for myself or for others. I feel reconnected. I feel complete.

Reflection Questions
What experience have you had that numbed you from feeling sadness?

What eventually allowed the tears to flow?

How has this impacted you and your connection to life experiences?

Mantra
**When I choose to allow tears to flow,
I honor who I am and what I feel.**

Whispers of your heart

_____

_____

_____

_____

_____

_____

_____

_____

_____

Fear

Fear comes in all shapes and sizes and does not discriminate. The reality is that the voice of fear becomes so familiar that it is more like white noise. You no longer hear it as an interruption or something that you are actually experiencing. Ruth Soukup, author of *Do It Scared*, confirms, "The reality is that most of our fear is happening subconsciously, inside our head, often without us realizing it, and without us recognizing that what we are feeling or experiencing is actually fear. Instead, we experience it as truth."[16] When you remember that fear is an emotion that needs to be felt and not a state of being, you are able to move through the fear and shift your perception. The more you understand your own fears, the more you are able to eliminate them.

Take a breath, be curious and allow the whispers of your heart to release your fears.

fear ...

solitary ... heavy ...

nagging ... swirling ... longing ...

rejection around the corner ...

overwhelm.

empty ... ominous ...

daunting ... grasping ... suffocating ...

craving answers and acceptance ...

surrender.

dark ... hollow ...

unsettling ... gripping ... paralyzing ...

seeking love to transform ...

growth.

Never trust your fears they don't know your strength.

—athena singh

When fear comes barreling into your world, you can easily become overwhelmed. You feel like you get steamrolled into submission; the old limiting beliefs creep back in from who knows where, and you doubt the very essence of what you are doing. After you take a deep breath and bring your hand to your heart center, you quiet the fear and self-doubt. Fear usually pops up as a reminder to tap into your strength and courage. The mind gets busy with all of the what-ifs, and you lose connection to the why. The fears aren't meant to dissuade you but to fan the flame within.

Reflection Questions
Describe a time when you felt overcome with fear and followed through anyway.

What was the end result of that experience?

What did you learn about yourself?

How does that help shift the lens of perception when you are witnessing someone else experiencing fear?

Mantra
**When I choose to lean into fear,
I gain strength.**

Of all the liars in the world, sometimes the worst are our own fears.

—Rudyard Kipling

The voice of fear is not only a liar—it can also drown out the whispers of the heart by the cacophony that accompanies it. Fear can create an immediate world of drama if believed and acted upon. It can stem from insecurities and low self-worth, leading down the dark, twisting rabbit hole. When fear pops up, be curious as to what's behind it. What's lingering in the dark that is holding you back? What false truth was planted and believed that is now ready to be gone? Fear can debilitate, or fear can inspire, depending on how you choose to react and respond.

Reflection Questions
Recall a time when you felt overcome by fear. Were you debilitated or inspired?

How did that situation resolve?

How might that situation have played out if the opposite response to fear was acted upon?

What did you learn about yourself?

Mantra
When I choose to be inspired by fear, I am courageous.

Everything you want is on the other side of fear.

—Jack Canfield

Fear is often the biggest roadblock you face in life. Fear kicks in, and the familiar tape loop of your weaknesses begins. If you are aware of your fears, you gain incredible strength as to how to move through the fear, using it to your advantage rather than a disadvantage. Knowing your fears provides clarity to what you need to move through. Even when fear seems overwhelming and paralyzing, lean in and be curious. Take a deep breath and ask yourself if what you are afraid of is real. Moving through the fear opens the door to what you long for.

Reflection Questions

What do you most want for yourself?

What fear story is playing on tape loop?

What do you need to believe instead?

Mantra

**When I choose to embrace what I want,
I weaken the grip of fear.**

Fears aren't facts; often they're just scary thoughts or feelings. Listen to what they have to say. When we're courageous enough to be with what scares us, we receive powerful wisdom.

—Kris Carr

Fear is an emotion that can feel overwhelming. The desire is to put on the tough outer coat and push through it, hoping you can force yourself through the fear or pretend that you're not afraid. Many have experienced moments of needing to move through a situation, be it at work or something similar, and still allow the fear to be felt. In those moments, it is helpful to have something in your toolbox to understand the nuts and bolts of fear. An acronym created to support leaning into fear is: **F**ully **E**mbracing **A**uthentic **R**eality. It is helpful to explore what seems real in the moment, even if the adult rational mind doesn't make sense of it. This exploration helps reveal the thoughts or feelings that open up the nuggets of wisdom.

Reflection Questions

Describe the last time you felt afraid.

What seemed real at that moment? What was the truth that was revealed?

How did that fear help you grow?

Mantra

When I choose to listen to what is behind fear, I change my relationship with fear.

Nothing in life is to be feared, it is only to be understood. Now is the time to understand more, so that we may fear less.

—Marie Curie

There are a variety of things that stir up fear: change, differences, judgment, overwhelm. Change is feared because there is so much unknown that awaits you. What will the end result be? Will I be able to handle it? Will it work? Naming what you're afraid of helps to soften that fear. Judgment of others who are different than you or who live lifestyles that don't reflect yours or make sense to you is another response to fear. Instead, open to the understanding that everyone makes the choices that feel most fitting to them, reflecting their life experiences, and allow that to be true for them. When you find yourself feeling afraid to embark on a new project, bring some understanding to what you fear. Once the fears are named, they weaken in power over you. When there is understanding and clarity, fear loses its grip.

Reflection Questions

What was the last thing, event, or person you were afraid of?

What needed to be understood in that moment?

How has that understanding influenced other areas or interactions in your life?

Mantra

**When I choose to understand,
I am open to life.**

Whispers of your heart

_____

_____

_____

_____

_____

_____

_____

_____

Courage

It takes courage to engage in living your life fully. Courage is that little whisper from the heart cheering you on when it feels like too much, facing the challenges to speak up and daring you to follow your dreams. And that's just the starting point. According to Lisa Dungate, PsyD, LMHC, and Jennifer Armstrong, courage can be categorized into six different types: physical, social, intellectual, moral, emotional, and spiritual. Different scenarios in your life inspire different types of courage.

Courage nudges you through fear, erases low self-esteem and dares you to risk. Kate Swoboda, creator of YourCourageousLife.com says, "Courage encompasses the ability to feel your fear without letting that fear dictate your options--in other words, the fear might be there, but you don't get stuck in it. I often think of courageous people as people who have decided to accept that fear will be along for the ride--but the fear has to ride in the passenger seat, not at the wheel steering where you go."[17]

Take a breath, be curious and courageously
listen to the whispers of your heart.

bold to say yes to your heart ...

confident in purpose and conviction ...

loving to the fullest extent ...

leading with pure intention ...

honoring faint whispers ...

a heart-inspired path ...

strength to shed the old ...

courage to believe.

We don't develop courage by being happy every day. We develop it by surviving difficult times and challenging adversity.

—Barbara De Angelis

Courage contains the Latin root cor, meaning "heart." Strength connected to heart. Speaking what's in your heart. Acting with guidance from the heart. Facing adversity with heart. Meeting opposition with heart. Standing firm in your truth rooted in the heart. Courage is like a muscle—the more you use it, the stronger it gets. When you are faced with adversity, you are being challenged to tap into your heart strength to find courage and remember what you are passionate about. Difficult times offer fuel to the inner fire, stirring up the courage to fight for what you believe in.

Reflection Questions
Recall a time when you were faced with adversity. Describe how you felt at that moment?

How did that adversity find resolution?

What did you learn about yourself from that experience?

Mantra
**When I choose to believe in myself,
I act with courage.**

Life shrinks or expands in proportion to one's courage.

—Anaïs Nin

When heart-centered strength is present in what you do, you tap into an endless source of inspiration and tenacity to grow and expand. It doesn't mean that there won't be stumbling blocks or setbacks along the way, but it does mean that there is a source of inner strength available to carry on. When you connect to your courage on a regular basis, it becomes more habitual and instinctive. Soon enough, it won't be a question of whether or not you can accomplish something but when it will be accomplished.

Reflection Questions

Describe a time when you thought you wouldn't make it through a situation or project.

What was the outcome?

How did you arrive at the outcome?

Mantra

When I choose to be courageous, my life is rich.

Take chances. Make mistakes. That's how you grow. Pain nourishes your courage. You have to fail in order to practice being brave.

—Mary Tyler Moore

Playing it safe leads to maintaining the status quo. But where is the richness in life if everything is predictable and within limited boundaries? How will you ever discover what your full potential is? What happens to curiosity and passion if chances aren't taken? There is a world of unknown and unfamiliar experiences waiting to be had to stir up the excitement in your heart. Mistakes inform you of what is still needed. It is the courageous heart that uses that information to attempt it again.

Reflection Questions

What was the last mistake you made that seemed disastrous?

How did you respond to it?

What did you learn about yourself from that mistake?

Mantra

**When I choose to explore life,
I discover the courage within.**

You will never do anything in this world without courage.

—Aristotle

Courage: heart-centered strength in the midst of conflict. In all reality, conflict happens daily. For example, there are goals for the day, and a phone call or email derails the entire plan. It takes courage to trust in the redirection and stay true to the attention and care needed. Or you wake up feeling a bit impatient and crabby. It takes courage to be gentle with yourself and allow those feelings to exist and move through in the time it takes it to do so. Without courage, either or both of those examples could lead to frustration, fear, or sadness paralyzing your response. Courage is the lifeline that supports daily living.

Reflection Questions

Think back to yesterday and a moment where your day was spontaneously redirected.

What was your response? How did you handle that moment?

How did your response serve you?

What did you learn from that moment?

Mantra

**When I choose to connect to courage,
my life flows with grace.**

What we face, we have the power to transform. What we ignore has the power to transform us.

—Ara

It's rarely easy to step into anything—pain, fear, shame, and so on—that has transformative power. Yet that transformation is the very reason you need to face what is before you. This brings to memory what I now refer to as "the great flood of 2008," where the massive storms that tore through my neighborhood left my tiny little house with an above-waist "pool" in the basement. I still have moments of wonder about how I made it through all of that, though my credit card bill is an all-too-real reminder! In all seriousness, the many layers involved in recovering from that incident proved to be transformational. I lived by myself and could have been defeated and sold the house with the thought that I don't have the ability to own and maintain a house on my own. Instead, I rallied up courage that I didn't realize was within me and continually faced every next thing that popped up along the way. And there were plenty. I rose to the challenge and lived alone in that house for another five years, tackling all that came my way with as much grace as I could muster. I learned of an unfamiliar amount of courage within me to face each new scenario, never doubting if I was going to make it. I can say with deep sincerity that I miss my little house. That house taught me more about myself than I could have ever imagined, and I continued to take care of it with all I had to offer. We were perfect for each other.

Reflection Questions

Reflect on a recent moment or event in your life that could have defeated you mentally, emotionally, or spiritually.

How did you handle that situation?

What did you learn about yourself in that process?

Is there a remaining element yet to be faced? If so, what is it?

What is behind the resistance to facing it?

Mantra

When I choose to face the challenge in front of me, I empower myself.

Whispers of your heart

_____

_____

_____

_____

_____

_____

_____

_____

Shame

Shame can be a highly charged emotion that can ravage and control what messages are replayed in your mind. It can stem from trauma or abuse experienced or the unpleasant result from a choice made. Shame may also result from forgetting something that was important to you or to someone you care about. There are no limits to what can trigger shame. The creator of The Trauma Therapist Podcast and Chief Clinical Officer at Seeking Integrity LLC, Robert Weiss, Ph.D., LCSW shares this about shame: "The natural reaction to shame is to hide it. So, most people isolate their shame and keep it secret. They push it down into the dark recesses of their soul, where it festers and tells them that they don't deserve to be happy, to be loved, or to succeed. Shame is like a vampire. It thrives in darkness; it dies in the light. Whenever, wherever, and however shame occurs, talking about it reduces its power, helping you progress from "I am bad" to "something bad happened."[18]

**Take a breath, be curious and bring
light to shame
through the whispers of your heart.**

Surviving Heinous Acts Meant to Exploit

Silencing Harmful Acts for Meaningful Evolution

Still Here After Mistakes Experienced

Spirit Holding Abundant Mercy Eternally

Strength, Healing, Acceptance Manifested Evermore

Shame has lost its power.

Where shame is, there is also fear.

—John Milton

Shame is connected to one's image of Self. If shame is present, fear of rejection is usually not far behind. Rejection then leads to fear of abandonment or being unlovable. This is a heavy burden to bear. The strongest way to face shame and move through it is to give voice to it. If the story connected to the shame is shared with a trusted person, the false beliefs around it will melt away. The truth of your value and worth will be revealed and healing can take place.

Reflection Questions

What life experience do you feel shame about?

What are the stories of fear that are held tightly within?

Be gentle with yourself in this process. This may be easier with professional guidance.

Mantra

**When I choose to honor my experiences,
I grow in courage and acceptance.**

If we can share our story with someone who responds with empathy and understanding, shame can't survive.

—Brené Brown

All it takes is one safe person. Just one. The story doesn't have to be broadcast for the world to hear. That's the power of one compassionate person. Sharing your stories frees your mind and opens your heart to loving yourself. When the stories are received with compassion, it reinforces the soul's knowledge of your inherent worth. The stories no longer hold the power of your hopes and dreams. The body finds a different space of balance and presence because the fear restriction around that story will be gone. It takes courage to share your story, but the reward is rich. It is also a call for you to be that one person for someone else, too. Remember that sometimes the one person is a professional therapist with experience in healing shame.

Reflection Questions
What story do you carry with you?

What belief is attached to that story?

What does the thought of sharing that story bring up within you?

Mantra
**When I choose to tell my story,
I am free of shame.**

Shame is the lie someone told you about yourself.

— Anaïs Nin

How many times have you heard the refrain "You should be ashamed of yourself" or "Shame on you"? Those statements can trigger plenty of memories, especially from childhood and young adulthood. When did something you did make you so shameful? When did the basic compassion of human connection lead to condemning the person instead of separating them from their actions or words? Those words of shame are often spoken by an authority figure, such as a parent, teacher, or coach. As a youngster, you believe the words spoken by those you look up to and are taught to respect. It is important to reclaim your sense of worthiness by letting go of the untrue beliefs thrust upon you.

Reflection Questions

Recall a moment when someone shamed you. What did that feel like?

Has there ever been a time where you shamed someone else? If so, what was behind that?

Mantra

**When I choose to accept my worth,
I see love.**

Once we realize that imperfect understanding is the human condition, there is no shame in being wrong, only in failing to correct our mistakes.

—George Soros

Making a mistake does not make you inferior or shameful. Mistakes open the door for honesty, integrity, and compassion. Taking responsibility for a mistake is powerful not only because the mistake is addressed, but also because your integrity is seen. Although the other may choose to respond in anger, that does not negate your integrity or bring about shame. The anger may indicate a level of discomfort in the vulnerability you demonstrated. The angry response is often what deters people from owning their mistakes more often. How do you respond to another when they take responsibility for a mistake? There is a deep level of self-compassion needed to take responsibility for a mistake and to know that this does not equate you to a bad person. The cycle of shame and accusations needs to be shifted into a pattern of compassion and acceptance.

Reflection Questions

Recall the last mistake you made, including who it affected and how you handled it.

What was the response to your mistake by other people?

What impact did their response have on you?

How can compassion and acceptance help?

Mantra

**When I choose to accept my mistakes,
I embrace who I am.**

Shame cannot exist in conditions of light, sunshine, and humor.
So the very moment that you share your most shameful
moments-and can learn to laugh about them—then the spell is
lifted. And you, too, are free.

—Christine Northrup

Love yourself through the shame. Always. There is nothing that makes anyone unlovable. Words and actions can be unlovable, but that doesn't mean you are. There is a significant difference between the two. When the shameful moment is shared with a trustworthy person, light and laughter can heal. There is relief in someone else staying present with you as you share and then opening to the vulnerability to express a moment of their own. Telling the story aloud rarely sounds as dreadful as it sounded in your head. All of the extra baggage and buildup that ego mind creates can all of a sudden be a bit humorous. And sometimes you need another person as a mirror to allow yourself to see it.

Reflection Questions

What shameful moment have you had the courage to share with another person?

How was it received?

How did it sound or appear to you as you were sharing it?

How did you feel after you shared your experience?

Mantra

When I choose to share my story,
I make room for laughter and joy.

Whispers of your heart

_____

_____

_____

_____

_____

_____

_____

_____

_____

Forgiveness

Forgiveness carries a mystique around it. You know that it is necessary and healing, yet you don't fully understand what it involves or how to do it. One aspect of forgiveness involves feeling the full range of emotions connected to the scenario, much like experiencing the different stages of grief. That aspect alone allows for a softening within and a willingness to open to releasing and forgiving. It is for your own well-being and peace of mind. Forgiveness is a choice, and you are responsible for it, even if you weren't the 'wrongdoer'. Holding a grudge and waiting for the other person to apologize isn't going to serve you. Greater Good Science Center at UC-Berkeley supports this by adding, "Psychologists generally define forgiveness as a conscious, deliberate decision to release feelings of resentment or vengeance toward a person or group who has harmed you, regardless of whether they actually deserve your forgiveness."[19]

Take a breath, be curious and open to forgiveness through the whispers of your heart.

Forgiveness

merciful ... compassionate ...

releasing ... healing ... freeing ...

deep understanding and acceptance ...

profound.

gracious ... vulnerable ...

deserving ... allowing ... welcoming ...

necessary freedom from chains ...

expansive.

sacred ... holy ...

transforming ... transmuting ... transcending ...

expression of Divine love ...

blessed.

Forgiveness is letting go of the hope that the past can be anything other than what it was.

—Unknown

I have found this concept to be a key element for me in working with forgiveness. Anytime I find myself unwilling to trust someone again, I realize I'm hanging on to something from the past, which could be as "past" as yesterday. The events that have already happened are not able to undo themselves. They happened. They're done. No do-overs. This won't erase the hurt, but it will soften the mind to allow for healing. I was taught a three-part process to assist in forgiving: compassion, acceptance, gratitude. There is no time frame assigned to this, only a matter of healing the heart. Compassion invites a softening around both parties involved, offering an openness to see a different perspective. Acceptance, not to be mistaken for complacency, is allowing the event to be a real occurrence, moving past the shock or shame of "I can't believe this happened!" Gratitude happens once the lessons involved or gained are seen and understood. There is often a slew of emotions that accompany this process, and it is important to allow them to be felt. The feeling deepens the healing.

Reflection Questions

What past hurt are you hanging onto?

Who does it involve?

Are you in need of forgiving yourself for anything? If so, for what?

Mantra

**When I choose to forgive,
I am free of the past.**

Forgiveness doesn't make the other person right; it makes you free.

—Stormie Omartian

As a young girl, I believed that forgiveness meant the actions of the other person were acceptable. I had no concept of it being about letting go of the words or the actions and moving on. I remember "forgiving" someone and then still being mad at them and carrying it around as a punishment to them, which was really a burden for me. As I got older, I found myself struggling a bit more with forgiveness. I really wanted to let things go but didn't quite understand how to do it. It felt like mental torture trying to navigate this whole forgiveness thing. I could tell myself that I forgave the other, but it didn't really sink into my heart and bring release. I have come to a deeper understanding of forgiveness that includes understanding my role in the situation and how my reactions may have contributed to the whole. This level of reflection has enabled my ability to forgive and let things go. In the event that I am still harboring resentment, I know that what has been triggered is my job to deal with and holding the other person accountable is unfair. This level of freedom opens my mind and heart.

Reflection Questions

What does forgiveness mean to you?

What is your relationship with forgiveness?

What, if anything, do you need to forgive yourself for?

Mantra

**When I choose to forgive,
I am more connected to life.**

Forgiveness is a sign that the person who has wronged you means more to you than the wrong they have dealt.

—Ben Greenhalgh

People make mistakes. When you are in need of forgiving another, it helps to shift perspective and change places. What if you are the wrongdoer in need of forgiveness? What would you want the other to do? The opportunity to forgive not only heals the relationship with the other, it also offers the chance for your own personal growth. The response to the wrongdoing can sometimes be out of proportion to the wrong itself. The event may trigger a different wound within you, and the other may end up taking responsibility for something they didn't do. Allow yourself to see beyond the wrong and connect to the person and then connect with your heart. This is where truth lies.

Reflection Questions

How has holding a grudge affected any relationships you are in or have been in?

What does that do to you emotionally?

What wound may have been triggered by the wrongdoing?

Mantra

**When I choose to forgive,
I gain self-awareness.**

Forgiveness is the key that unlocks the door of resentment and the handcuffs off hatred. It is a power that breaks the chains of bitterness and the shackles of selfishness.

—Corrie Ten Boom

Forgiveness reflects a level of self-worth. When worth and self-esteem are present, forgiveness has a better chance of being accessible. Grudges can be held because you are seeking acknowledgment of your worth. The wrongdoing is viewed from a desire for external approval. "If you really cared about me, then you wouldn't have _____." Attachment to external approval yields greater resistance to forgiveness. When you can move beyond the external need and develop the internal acceptance, forgiveness becomes more accessible and clearer vision, guided by compassion, can move in.

Reflection Questions

Reflect on a person in your life that you need to forgive. What are you holding onto?

What do you want the other person to see or acknowledge about you?

What role does your own self-esteem play in this scenario?

Mantra

**When I choose to forgive,
I deepen my self-worth.**

To forgive is the highest, most beautiful form of love. In return, you will receive untold peace and happiness.

—Robert Muller

Forgiveness is seeing beyond the wrong and loving the soul underneath it all. Hanging on to wrongdoing is toxic and poisonous to the soul. Even in the case of wrongful deaths and serious crimes, forgiveness is still needed. Anything that taints the heart has lasting damage beyond the wrongdoing, even closing your heart to loving those in your life who you really do love. It even leads to greater fear around love, placing all sorts of rules and expectations as to how it should be in order for you to feel safe enough to love. Regardless of the severity of the wrongdoing, forgiveness releases the poison and offers healing for all.

Reflection Questions
What is your resistance to forgiveness?

What do you believe will happen if you do/don't forgive someone?

Mantra
**When I choose to be vulnerable and forgive,
I open myself to healing.**

Whispers of your heart

_____

_____

_____

_____

_____

_____

_____

_____

Pain

Pain, be it physical, emotional, mental, or spiritual, is a manifestation of an energy blockage within. The International Association for the Study of Pain includes "an unpleasant sensory and emotional experience" as part of its definition of pain. It's your body's way of getting you to slow down, pay attention and acknowledge what you are feeling. Pain is a love nudge to notice your body in a gentle, compassionate way instead of making it a slave to the will of the mind. Being mindful of emotions and physical sensations alleviates the desire to be wrapped up in the pain experience. It also shifts the need to use pain as a cry for attention from another person. When you are responsible for paying attention to your own needs, the attachment to pain loses its grip. Open yourself to exploring all aspects of pain—physical, emotional, mental and spiritual.

Take a breath, be curious and hear
your pain through the whispers of your heart.

Help me know the pain, this aching in my heart.
Help me know the truth that I have known from the start.

Help me hear the stories that are held so deep within.
Help me hear the answers to guide the place where I begin.

Help me touch the wounds that seek love and gentle care.
Help me touch the depths of the burdens that I bear.

Help me see the beauty of Your day-to-day embrace.
Help me see Your presence in every passing face.

Help me taste the richness of every passing moment.
Help me taste the sweetness of the beauty of my life.

Pain is the great teacher of mankind. Beneath its breath, souls develop.

—Marie von Ebner-Eschenbach

Everyone has experienced pain at some point in their life, be it physical, mental, emotional or spiritual. What is done with the pain determines the development that follows. A common response to any form of pain is to constrict and brace against it, which only increases resistance. Pain is not a comfortable feeling but one that holds much wisdom. One of the first steps in dealing with pain is to breathe, allowing the body to find as much ease within the pain as possible. Have no agenda with the breath other than allowing the mind and body to find peace and trust being in the moment. Pain can be quite complex at times, holding many layers of information. What manifests as physical pain may reveal itself to be emotional pain. Regardless of how the pain manifests to the conscious mind, open to it. Build a relationship between the mind and body; let them communicate with each other to grow, heal and develop.

Reflection Questions
What pain are you currently experiencing?

What layers are underneath it?

How can you go about offering healing to your body?

Mantra
**When I choose to acknowledge pain,
I heal.**

You feel your strength in the experience of pain.

—Jim Morrison

When you really lean into pain, you find that you are stronger than you think you are. Pain ignites the flame of survival and rising above, like a phoenix. Pain holds transformative power when you use it as a teacher, even when the message is simply to slow down. For many, slowing down or taking time off is a sign of weakness or being unproductive. However, pain reminds you to tend to the very being that allows for you to be here and experience life at all. It takes mental and emotional strength to slow down and listen. Strength is rarely about physical strength. Pain opens your awareness to the mental, emotional and spiritual strength within you. Are you willing to ask for guidance and help, beyond just taking the pain away? Do you believe in your own strength to move through the pain?

Reflection Questions

What is your familiar response to pain?

How does that serve you?

What would it look or feel like to lean into the pain?

Mantra

**When I choose to learn from pain,
I gain emotional, mental, and spiritual strength.**

Pain is inevitable. Suffering is optional.

—Haruki Murakami

Pain is one of life's valuable teachers. It challenges you to dig deeper and discover strength you don't think you have. It shows you where you are getting stuck in limiting beliefs. It is the barometer for when you need to slow down and take care of yourself. Even though pain is uncomfortable, it is an expected part of growth. You need to understand what is holding you back and use the information as you move forward. Lean into the pain, learn from it, and allow the nuggets to guide you forward. If you choose to hang onto the pain, ignoring it, resisting it, pushing through it, it turns into suffering. If you are not careful, an attachment is formed to the suffering, and it erroneously becomes part of your identity. You become a perceived victim of your pain, and the same thoughts continually run through your mind.

Reflection Questions
What is your belief about pain?

What is your belief about suffering?

How can either or both of those be shifted to support leaning into feeling pain?

Mantra
**When I choose to lean into pain,
I gain pearls of wisdom about myself.**

Your pain is the breaking of the shell that encloses your understanding.

—Kahlil Gibran

Pain. A feeling many would rather ignore, be it physical or emotional. Whenever you find yourself pulling away from feeling pain, use one of two acronyms to give you a love nudge: **P**ay **A**ttention **I**nward **N**ow and **P**urposely **A**ccessing **I**nner **N**eeds. Either way you look at it, the invitation is to slow down and be curious about what is going on within. Although the exploration can be messy and uncomfortable, the nuggets discovered are well worth it.

Reflection Questions

Recall a time when you were experiencing pain, either physical or emotional.

What was your reaction to the pain?

How did you tend to it?

How did that serve you?

What information did you gain about yourself from that experience?

Mantra

**When I acknowledge and listen to my pain,
I build a deeper understanding of myself.**

Pain is never permanent.

—Teresa of Ávila

This is an affirmation that can be used to guide the mind and body into ease, releasing the grip of fear that is attached to the pain. Healing occurs when the mind and body are most at peace, surrendering and allowing the natural process to take place. Pain seems more permanent when you attach to it mentally. Do you keep your focus and attention on your pain, or do you breathe into the pain and allow it to exist without trying to control it? Be mindful and gentle with what you are experiencing, free of resistance and rigidity. Be curious about what fear is being triggered. Lean in, learn, and let go.

Reflection Questions
What prevents you from leaning into pain?

What have you learned from the pain you have felt?

How did it feel to allow your body to release the pain without controlling it?

Mantra
**When I choose to be free of attachment to pain,
I find peace with greater ease**

Whispers of your heart

_____

_____

_____

_____

_____

_____

_____

_____

Self-Worth

Self-worth is your personal sense of value, the core of who you are. It affects your confidence, self-esteem, and overall emotional balance. You typically determine your self-worth by personal evaluation or comparison to the worth of others. It is subjective yet links deeply into your personal power. If you don't believe in your own worthiness, you end up feeling powerless. Dr. Christina Hibbert, PsyD and specialist in motherhood and women's mental health, shares that self-worth "is a deep knowing that I am of value, that I am loveable, necessary to this life, and of incomprehensible worth."[20]

Take a breath, be curious and explore your self-worth in the whispers of your heart.

Stop doing. Stop proving.
Stop comparing. Stop demanding.

It is all unnecessary.

You are worthy because you are. You do enough.
You are enough. You love enough. You forgive enough.
You serve enough. You know enough.
You are talented enough. You are pretty enough.

You are enough.

Embrace your you.

Embrace the goofy things that make you giggle even
though nobody else laughs. Embrace the touching
things that bring tears to your eyes. Embrace the
knowledge you have that may seem useless to other
people. Embrace the quirky things that fascinate you.
Embrace the past that helped inform who you are
today.

Embrace the unique magnificence that resides
within you.

Your past mistakes are meant to guide you, not define you.

—Positive Energy Plus

It is all too easy to keep the proverbial punishing stick in your hands and beat yourself up for mistakes you have made. Because you have free choice, you are bound to make mistakes, rub people the wrong way, disappoint people, and even fall flat on your face. However, part of your free choice gives you the opportunity to be curious about what happened, to see where or how the slip happened rather than the end result. You get stuck in the "I should've" instead of how to use the information to guide you. It is the innocence of mistakes that teaches you from a very young age. When you were young and told not to touch the hot stove, you learned the lesson best by touching the hot stove and experiencing how much it hurt. You could either see yourself as a disobedient child or one who has learned that it hurts to touch a hot stove and not to do it again. Mistakes translate into experience and knowledge—if you allow for it to happen.

Reflection Questions

What mistake have you made that you keep beating yourself up about?

What did you learn from that experience?

How has that mistake/lesson guided you?

Mantra

When I choose to be curious about my mistakes, I gain experience and knowledge.

Someone's opinion of you does not have to become your reality.

—Les Brown

Know your value. Know your worth. Own them both deeply within your heart. When you believe in your own value and worth, other people don't carry as much influence on your perception of you. When you find yourself getting wrapped up in someone else's opinion of you, be curious enough to ask yourself why. There are people who you come across in the course of a day who don't impact your sense of worth. Then there are the people whose reactions or opinions can broadside you and turn on the mental monkey chatter. It's important to understand what significance those particular people have in your life and what you most fear surrounding their reactions to you. Then you can reclaim your sense of worth and empower yourself.

Reflection Questions

Who in your life experience can trigger a space of unworthiness?

What importance do they carry in your life?

Why is their opinion so important?

Mantra

**When I choose to know my worth,
I empower myself.**

Whatever you consistently attach to the words "I am," you will become.

—Zig Ziglar

The words you choose have a large impact on your sense of self-worth.
 "I am sad."
 "I am ugly."
 "I am depressed."
 "I am stupid."
 "I am unlovable."

Although you may feel sad, you are not sadness. You may feel stupid (i.e., embarrassed), but that does not make you stupid. There may be thoughts that this is all a play on semantics, which it is, but it has an impact. "I am" creates an attachment or a label that becomes personal, where "I feel" describes a sensation or an experience. The attachment can then create an expectation or limiting experience that can easily lead down the dark rabbit hole, whereas "I feel" allows the sensation to pass. The key is in the awareness, actually hearing what you say. And, yes, this applies to what you say about yourself in your head, too.

Reflection Questions
How often do you really listen to what you say?

When was the last time you used "I am" followed by something perceived as negative (like the examples above)?

What did you say?

Did you believe it to be true?

What triggered the comment?

Mantra
**When I choose to be aware of the words I use,
I speak through love.**

The reason we struggle with insecurity is because we compare our behind-the-scenes with everyone else's highlight reel.

—Steven Furtick

Social interactions are largely based on the surface-level successes of life. Unless you are with close friends, conversation doesn't tend to go much deeper than that. If it's not personal successes, then it is the success of the spouse, children, or even grandchildren. Most people don't waste an opportunity to share a multitude of amazing things that they or someone they know have accomplished. It can be overwhelming to listen to, especially if it is a day where your biggest success was making it out of bed. The internal judgment reel starts, and the closest opportunity to bow out of the conversation is being sought. As someone who finds it challenging to start random conversations, I can easily become mentally paralyzed and forget anything and everything. This is an even greater struggle with the popularity of social media, which thrives on the ability to project living a perfect life. There are constant postings of vacations, successes, meals and nights out on the town, showcasing the highlight reel. Social media is an easy and dangerous trap to get entangled in, leaving a feeling of emptiness and sadness.

Reflection Questions

How would you describe your comfort level in social settings?

How do you direct conversation?

Are you the highlight reel or the behind-the-scenes person?

What nugget can you take to your next social engagement?

Mantra

**When I accept my life,
I am at peace.**

There is no perfection, only beautiful versions of brokenness.
—Shannon L. Alder

This quote is a poignant reminder that you are here navigating life as gracefully as possible, creating and revising the map as you go. Nobody has all of the answers. You have different experiences that lead to different answers and different ideas. Brokenness doesn't mean that you need fixing. It is the idea that you are trying to make sense of the experiences you have lived and see how that continually creates and recreates who you are. Perfection doesn't allow for revision and tweaking; growth does. Embrace what you bring to every moment of every day, knowing that it is valuable because it comes from you. Even on the days when that feels like a stretch, remind yourself anyway.

Reflection Questions

How do you see yourself?

How would you describe your sense of worth?

How does this affect how you perceive others?

How much pressure do you place on yourself to be perfect?

Mantra

**When I choose to see the beauty of who I am,
I see my worthiness.**

Whispers of your heart

_____

_____

_____

_____

_____

_____

_____

_____

Feelings

Feelings are the key to healing yet the very thing you'd prefer to avoid. You are inadvertently taught from young on to ignore or get over your feelings. "But avoiding unpleasant emotions--rather than accepting them--only increases our psychological distress, inflexibility, anxiety, and depression, diminishing our well-being,"[21] shares Dr. Beth Kurland, a clinical psychologist and author. When you accept your own feelings, it becomes easier to accept how others feel. It also helps to understand that emotions are energy in motion, creating sensations within the body and that the feelings you feel are unique to you based on your own experiences.

Take a breath, be curious and discover your feelings in the whispers of your heart.

I am who I am.
I feel what I feel.

I don't need you to fix me. I need you to see me.
I don't need you to cower away in your own fear.
I need you to sit vulnerably with me.

I don't need you to understand why.
I need you to accept what is.

I don't need you to change it.
I need your companionship while it passes.

I don't need your limited understanding.
I need your open mind and heart.

I don't need your judgment.
I need your acceptance.

See me.
In my emotional vulnerability,
See me.

Our feelings are our most genuine paths to knowledge.

—Audre Lorde

Your feelings are unique to you. No one else is going to have the exact same reaction or emotional response to a situation like you. There may be similarities among others, but none that are exactly the same. Your feelings are uniquely yours, based on your own experiences. When you choose to honor your feelings, you choose to deepen your relationship with your experiences and understand how they can inform and shape your life. There is a world of knowledge and wisdom within you if you choose to feel it.

Reflection Questions

How does it feel when you are with a group of people and the majority respond to a situation differently than you do?

What is behind your response?

What did you learn about yourself in that moment?

Mantra

**When I choose to honor my feelings,
I am at ease within myself.**

Emotions are not right or wrong, good or bad. They are merely indicators of what is happening, and what must be listened to, usually in the body. People who do not feel deeply finally do not know or love deeply either.

—Fr. Richard Rohr

You have been inadvertently taught how to disregard your emotions. It is important for that to change, for you to learn how to understand what you are feeling. Part of this process includes paying enough attention to the body to slow down and be curious. Your body lets you know when something has been triggered within, ranging anywhere from sweating and tension to nausea and being antsy. The more you pay attention, the more you understand the messages from the body. The more you understand the messages, the more you can learn about yourself. As the relationship to your own self deepens in acceptance, the same can then be offered to other people.

Reflection Questions

How do you feel, using one of these six words: sad, mad, glad, hurt, ashamed, afraid?

Where do you feel that in your body? Describe that feeling.

Leaning into that, what could be behind that?

How can this information be helpful to you?

Mantra

**When I choose to feel my emotions,
I connect more fully to those around me.**

Allow the emotion to dissolve so the energy trapped within it is released and blossoms as wisdom.

—Tsoknyi Rinpoche

Emotions are energy in motion. When you choose not to feel them, you are increasing the pressure within because the energy that wants to move is being blocked. There is an ease at coming up with reasons not to feel your feelings:

· "It's not the right time."
· "It's not the right place."
· "They are going to think I'm weak."
· "I don't understand where this is coming from."
· "They're going to think I'm depressed."

However, one good cry and things seem better almost immediately. The release of the emotion, in this case, through a good cry, could create a different sense of clarity around a situation or an awareness of a limiting belief ready to be released. Emotions offer you the opportunity to peel back the layers and be curious about what is going on behind them.

Reflection Questions
Recall a time when you experienced strong emotion. Describe it as fully as you can, recalling how your physical body felt in the moment too.

How did you work your way through that emotion?

What did you discover behind it?

How have you been able to use that discovery since that time?

Mantra

When I choose to be curious about my emotions, I gain nuggets of wisdom about myself.

You can't discover genuine self-love until you exercise radical honesty with your true feelings.

—Kelly McNelis,
Your Messy Brilliance: 7 Tools for the Perfectly Imperfect Woman

Feelings are often met with fear and resistance. Generally speaking, you are not taught how to feel your feelings while growing up, leaving you deficient in this area as an adult. A common reaction to feelings is to push them down as far as possible, pretending they don't exist. Eventually, you run out of room, leaving no option but to release, and there can be a lot of fear as to what that will look like. You can start by identifying how you're feeling: "I feel sad. I feel angry. I feel hurt." This opens the door to what you are sensing in your body and extends an invitation to be curious. Sometimes a simple cry, your built-in, natural reset button, will do the trick. Yet sometimes you need to delve more into what is behind the feelings. What is causing these feelings to arise? Oftentimes, the answer that comes up opens the door to deeper healing. This gentleness and curiosity foster a deeper relationship with yourself and encourages greater self-love.

Reflection Questions

Describe the most recent time you had a heightened emotional response to someone or something.

Be curious and ask what was behind that emotion. What limiting belief could be behind the scenes?

When have you experienced this belief before?

How can you use this nugget to bring a new perspective to light?

Mantra

**When I am curious about my feelings,
I gain deeper awareness.**

Nothing destroys self-worth, self-acceptance, and self-love faster than denying what you feel. Without feelings, you would not know where you are in life. Nor would you know what areas you need to work on. Honor your feelings. Allow yourself to feel them.

—Iyanla Vanzant

Feelings have somehow gotten a bad reputation. Witnessing people experiencing their emotions tends to make others uncomfortable and even judgmental. The reality lies in the knowledge that feelings carry raw truth, be it lessons to learn, releasing limiting beliefs or healing past wounds. It's often the "raw" part that repels people away from feeling. Yet the "raw" is what opens you to seeing and experiencing your own truth. Through your feelings, you are given the opportunity to open yourself to life, to experience the richness of learning about yourself and to use that information to connect with others. You can build a relationship with yourself by honoring your feelings.

Reflection Questions

Take a deep breath and check in with yourself. How are you feeling (sad, mad, glad, hurt, ashamed, afraid)?

Allow yourself to be curious about your answer. What is behind that emotion?

What nugget of truth is there to be gained behind that emotion?

Mantra

**When I choose to feel my feelings,
I honor who I am.**

Whispers of your heart

_____

_____

_____

_____

_____

_____

_____

_____

Love

Love is an emotional connection to someone or something. In order to love, you need to accept the person or thing as they are, even the aspects that can crawl under your skin. There is full acceptance of who the other person is even when there is behavior you don't like. Psychologist Dr. Barbara Fredrickson states, "Love is primarily about connection, and it is important to our health and happiness, affecting our brains and bodies at the cellular level."[22]

The ability and depth of loving others is reflected by your ability to love yourself. Katie Beecher, a medical intuitive, shares, "According to a dictionary definition of "love," it is a profoundly tender, passionate affection for another person. Self-love, then, would be a passionate affection for ourselves. It is treating ourselves the way we would treat people we truly love: with tenderness, understanding, and compassion in our actions and words."[23]

Take a breath, be curious and discover love in the whispers of your heart.

I ache to be

seen,

heard,

acknowledged,

respected,

desired,

accepted,

valued,

savored …

… and I am going to offer it to myself.

I don't need to wait until

I lose weight,

make more money,

color my hair,

am more confident,

meet the "right" person,

change my quirky habits.

I am loved for who I am.

Right now.

Oh, what we find when we stop searching. Oh, what we feel when we stop forcing. Oh, what we receive when we stop fearing. Oh, what we become when we just love.

—Creig Crippen

Love. Be present. Accept. Listen. Witness. Savor. Feel. Breathe. Slow down. Receive. Give. Openness. Mutuality. Respect. Vulnerability. Care. Compassion. Gratitude. Connection. Take in what is in front of you instead of wishing it were different. Notice the sensations of what you are experiencing instead of pushing through. Know and believe in your worthiness instead of wondering how others perceive you. See beyond the words and deeds and choose love.

Reflection Questions

What do you see in your space right now? Take it all in. What can you be grateful for within your current space?

How do you feel right now? What do you need to pay attention to?

What was the last thing you allowed yourself to receive from somebody else?

What would it be like for you to always choose love?

Mantra

When I choose to slow down and be present, I experience love.

Instructions for living a life: Pay attention. Be astonished. Tell about it.

—Mary Oliver

This quote embraces love. When you love life, you pay attention to everything: other people, animals, nature, and everything in between. Love allows you to be astonished by all that you see, feel, hear, and experience. Love invites you to embrace the unique and diverse aspects of others. Love encourages you to share your experience so others are willing to do the same. Love softens how you see the interconnectedness of all things.

Reflection Questions

Think of a person with whom you are very close, be it a spouse, partner, friend, or family member.

When was the last time you really paid attention to them?

When were you last astonished by them, be it something they said or something they did?

When was the last time you shared that with them?

Repeat these questions in connection to nature or with anything else that comes to mind.

Mantra

**When I choose to be present,
I experience life through the lens of love.**

The most important thing in life is to learn how to give out Love, and to let it come in.

—Morrie Schwartz

On the surface, love seems like such a simple concept, but it is deep and rich in action. **L**anguage **O**f **V**ulnerable **E**xperiences. When you choose to give out love, it is connected to acceptance and openness, which can be a very vulnerable experience. To let love come in, you need to have some level of self-worth, which can also be vulnerable. Giving and receiving love requires vulnerability and acceptance. The freedom from expectations invites an openness to the other person, creating a path for love to flow.

Reflection Questions

What do you notice in your body when you embrace the idea of receiving love?

What belief do you have around giving out love? About receiving love?

How easy is it for you to give out love to random people you encounter throughout your day? To coworkers? To friends? To family?

Mantra

**When I choose to experience love,
I find joy.**

But love, I've come to understand, is more than three words mumbled before bedtime. Love is sustained by action, a pattern of devotion in the things we do for each other every day.

—Nicholas Sparks

Love is far more than the fairy tale you grow up with or what you create as a way of escaping the challenges you face. Love includes loving who you are when you are with a person who loves you in return. It is an unending flow of loving yourself and loving another. They feed each other constantly. If you struggle with some aspect of yourself, you will likely notice it in the one you love and find yourself criticizing it in them, without realizing you do the same thing. Then love steps in and allows for the safety around your struggles, softening and opening. Love is a divine gift that offers the opportunity to honor each other and yourself without wanting or expecting anything in return. Love is the desire to allow the partnership to flourish in ways beyond your control.

Reflection Questions
How do you allow for vulnerability to be present when you love someone?

How do you sustain love through action and devotion?

Mantra
**When I choose to have love as a guide,
I am sustained by love.**

Let us love ourselves so fiercely that when others see us, they know exactly how it should be done.

—Rudy Francisco

It often seems easier to love others than to truly love yourself. You can get stuck in the weeds of self-judgment, entangled in the web of worthiness, and turned upside down by pleasing others. Loving yourself includes deep acceptance of all parts of you: the past that you'd rather forget, the quirks that make you unique, the amazingness of your talents, the hobbies that fill your hearts, and the forgiveness still waiting to occur. The tendency is to pick and choose what you love about yourself and when it is acceptable to do so. Love it all. Right now. Always. Every part of who you are and every experience you have had help create and inform the person you are today. Allow yourself to be amazed with yourself every single day.

Reflection Questions
Name a quality about yourself that you love. How do you foster this aspect of you every day?

What aspect of yourself do you find yourself getting irritated with? How can you soften around that?

Mantra
**When I choose to love all of me,
I am whole.**

Whispers of your heart

_____

_____

_____

_____

_____

_____

_____

_____

Passion

Passion is a strong emotion of desire or enthusiasm for a person or an activity. It's someone or something that inspires the fire in the belly and a motivation to devote time and energy. Psychologist Darrell Franklin describes, "Passion is a specific kind of motivation that comes from something that someone believes is part of them and helps them create their identity or meaning in their life."[24] It is something that feeds the soul and feels richly fulfilling to engage in. If you feel you are lacking passion, take notice of how busy you are. Allow time to engage in the activities that nurture your soul.

Take a breath, be curious and awaken
your passion with the whispers of your heart.

Trapped by fears and daunting pressure to fit in, you swirl in agonizing misery and long to break free.

You search for self-expression in everything you do, yet feel you come up short.

Defeated.

Ridiculed.

Exasperated.

Empty.

The longing, aching, and yearning of your heart are increasingly alive, begging to be heard and daring you to listen.

You want to say yes, but fear tells you to play it safe.

But why?

For who?

For how long?

Take the risk.

Say yes to your heart, to your soul.

You don't have to know the answers.

Just say yes.

Everything you need is within you even more than you can imagine.

Each of us has a fire in our hearts for something. It's our goal in life to find it and keep it lit.

—Mary Lou Retton

There's often a lot of talk and musing around your purpose in life. You can get lost in the wonder and look for the "right path" that will lead you there. What if your purpose was exactly this—to find the fire in your heart and keep it lit? Finding the fire in your heart will continually lead you where you need to go. Keeping it lit is the reminder to check in daily to see where you go or what you do next. You have all of the answers you need within you. You know what you love, what inspires you, and what you're good at. What you often need to learn is how to connect the dots.

Reflection Questions
What is the fire in your heart?

What do you do to fan the fire and keep it lit?

What limiting beliefs or old stories arise when you connect to what you're passionate about?

Mantra
When I choose to engage in what I'm passionate about, I lead an inspired life.

All I insist on, and nothing else, is that you should show the whole world that you are not afraid.

—W. A. Mozart

Let your passion be stronger than your fear. Avoid getting wrapped in the worries and the what-ifs. All they do is dampen the fire of the passion and steer you away from what you really want. Let your passion ignite the commitment to follow through and rise above the fear. Fear can creep up, but understand it and use it to your advantage. Behind the scenes is where the true nuts-and-bolts work happens, where passion fuels the work and feeds the soul. And when the time comes for your work to be seen, hold nothing back. Connect to the very same passion that has been feeding you and let it shine. Do not let the fear hold you back or make you shy away from being seen in your glory and passion.

Reflection Questions
What happens when you have the opportunity to let yourself be seen?

How much do you allow your passion to be present in all that you do?

What prevents you from letting your passion be your guide?

Mantra
**When I choose to connect to my passion,
I am seen for who I am.**

Death is not the greatest loss in life. The greatest loss is what dies inside us while we live.

—Norman Cousins

Life without connection to passion. It sounds so drastic, but it happens daily. You find your routine that brings comfort and structure and rarely go beyond that space. Even though you may enjoy what you do, it doesn't always mean that there is connection and passion involved. It's easy to become little robots, disengaged from the emotional connection to your work. You become so caught up in routine that you forget why you do what you do. And if your work doesn't offer that connection, it is vital to your well-being to have something that does fan the fire in the belly. Connect to the why every day—and may it be more engaging than the paycheck.

Reflection Questions

Why do you have the job that you do?

What emotional connection does it offer you?

What other activities are you involved in?

How do they feed your passion?

Mantra

When I choose to connect with my passion, I feel fulfilled.

Take time to reclaim your creativity and watch your life blossom as a result.

—Madisyn Taylor

Oftentimes when you feel stuck, it is due to not being connected to what inspires you. Life becomes static and predictable, allowing for more opportunities to "check out" and not be engaged. This type of numbness within the day-to-day can even lead to not really recalling what happened during the day. Creativity doesn't have to be something out of the ordinary. Creativity can be changing up what you eat at mealtime, wearing bolder colors that you normally wouldn't wear, taking a new way home from work, or even listening to a different radio station. It's the little things that re-engage the creative mind and bring a revived energy to the day.

Reflection Questions

What do you do to engage your creative mind?

How can that be expanded?

What holds you back from using your creative mind?

Mantra

**When I choose to engage my creativity,
I am energized.**

Every great dream begins with a dreamer. Always remember you have within you the strength, the patience, and the passion to reach for the stars and change the world.

—Harriet Tubman

When you open your heart and mind and allow the intention of the dream to align, all things are possible. Time presents itself. The skills are readily available. The mountains seem more like anthills. The balance with the rest of your life is in check. The passion is ignited and stays strong until the dream is reached. It feels like you're donning a superhero cape and you can conquer anything and everything. Know your dream. Breathe life into your dream. Build a relationship with your dream and vow to nurture it until it blooms.

Reflection Questions

What do you dream of doing?

What needs to happen to open and align your heart and mind?

What would it feel like to change the world?

Mantra

When I choose to open my heart and mind to my dreams, I succeed.

Whispers of your heart

_____

_____

_____

_____

_____

_____

_____

_____

Divine Spirit, I seek your wisdom.

Teach me to appreciate the gifts of this life.

Teach me to accept all of me,
especially what I judge as unlovable.

Teach me to forgive so I may have a pure heart.

Teach me to speak truth with gentleness and compassion.

Teach me to see the blessings that surround me every day.

Teach me to be aware of the unspoken message I convey.

Teach me to fully develop the talents I have been gifted.

Teach me to risk the unknown and listen to my soul.

Teach me to find laughter and joy in every day.

Teach me to crave knowledge with childlike curiosity.

Teach me to be a vessel for Your light and love.

Teach me to savor stillness to hear
the whispers of my heart.

Works Cited

1. Wauters, Ambika. The Book of Chakras. Quarto, 2002.

2. Judith, Anodea. Eastern Body Western Mind. Celestial Arts, 1996, 2004.

3. Falchuk, Aimee. "Understanding How to Move and Manipulate Energy." 1 April 2020, https://goop.com/wellness/mindfulness/understanding-how-to-move-and-manipulate-energy/

4. Lamott, Anne. Help, Thanks, Wow. Riverhead Books, 2001.

5. Gerst, Alena. "3 Ways Prayers Can Help You Heal." 30 December 2013, https://www.mindbodygreen.com/0-12073/3-ways-prayers-can-help-you-heal.html

6. Hassler, Christine. Expectation Hangover: Overcoming Disappointment in Work, Love, and Life. New World Library, 2014.

7. Randall-Young, Gwen. "The Importance of Being Heard." 1 April 2020, http://gwen.ca/the-importance-of-being-heard/

8. Alexander, Ronald, Dr. Wise Mind, Open Mind: Finding Purpose and Meaning in Times of Crisis, Loss, and Change. New Harbinger Publications, 2009

9. Finley, Guy. "For the Judgy Among Us: 6 Things that Happen Every Time You Judge Someone". 28 June 2019, https://www.mindbodygreen.com/articles/why-judging-others-is-bad-for-us-and-how-to-stop-being-judgmental

10. Cobb, Ellie, PhD. "How to Feel More Connected to Yourself & Others". 19 August 2019, https://www.mindbodygreen.com/articles/how-to-connect-better-with-others-and-yourself-for-better-health

11. Kaiser, Shannon. "5 Practices for Couples Seeking to Deepen Their Connection." 13 February 2019, https://www.mindbodygreen.com/articles/couples-deepen-connection

12. Gonsalves, Kelly. "Why We Need to Rethink the Way We Talk About Anger." 14 May 2019, https://www.mindbodygreen.com/articles/types-of-anger-gender-and-why-you-dont-need-to-stop-feeling-angry

13. MacDonald, Cheryl A., Dr. "Is there a Relationship between Happiness and Joy?" 1 April 2020, https://healthpsychology.org/is-there-a-relationship-between-happiness-and-joy/

14. Anwar, Yasmin. "How the GGSC Helped Turn Pixar "Inside Out": Greater Good Science Center director Dacher Keltner scientific advice to Pixar's new family film." 19 June 2015, https://greatergood.berkeley.edu/article/item/how_ggsc_turned_pixar_inside_out

15. Forgas, Joseph P., PhD. "Four Ways Sadness May Be Good for You". 4 June 2014, https://greatergood.berkeley.edu/article/item/four_ways_sadness_may_be_good_for_you

16. Soukup, Ruth. "The 7 Fear Archetypes & How to Figure Out Yours." 21 May 2019, https://www.mindbodygreen.com/articles/ruth-soukup-seven-fear-archetypes-descriptions-and-how-to-figure-out-yours

17. Swoboda, Kate. "7 Habits that Build Courage (and a Better Life)." 19 May 2019, https://www.mindbodygreen.com/articles/7-habits-that-build-courage-and-a-better-life

18. Weiss, Robert, PhD, MSW. "How to Let Go of Your Deepest Shame-For Good." 2 April 2020, https://www.mindbodygreen.com/0-26377/how-to-let-go-of-your-deepest-shame-for-good.html

19. UC-Berkeley, Greater Good Science Center. "What is Forgiveness?" 2 April 2020, https://greatergood.berkeley.edu/topic/forgiveness/definition

20. Ackerman, Courtney. "What is Self-Worth and How Do We Increase It?" 7 April 2019, https://positivepsychology.com/self-worth

21. Kurland, Beth. "What Happens When You Embrace Dark Emotions." 14 January 2019, https://greatergood.berkeley.edu/article/item/what_happens_when_you_embrace_dark_emotions

22. Suttie, Jill. "The Love Upgrade." 4 February 2013, https://greatergood.berkeley.edu/article/item/the_love_upgrade

23. Beecher, Katie. "Using Intuition to Find Self-Acceptance." 2 April 2020, https://goop.com/wellness/spirituality/using-intuition-to-find-self-acceptance/

24. Franklin, Darrell. "What is the Psychology of Passion?" 19 June 2015, https://www.quora.com/What-is-the-psychology-of-passion

About Lux Eterna Healing

Lux Eterna Healing is the auspice under which I hold my energy healing practice. Lux Eterna (loox ā-tair-nă) is Latin for "light eternal," representing the light of the soul that shines forever. It is a gentle landing place where love-light, curiosity and awareness blend to inspire spiritual growth.

My inspiration as an intuitive energy and crystal healer is to share the tools I have learned and used on my own personal journey to guide your healing, releasing what is holding you back from feeling fulfilled and connected in your day to day life. I use the information received from the energy in your body to guide your transformation from the inside out. You gain awareness about your patterns and how they affect you physically, mentally, emotionally and spiritually. The energy work aids in the physical release of those patterns and empowers you and informs the choices you make.

At the risk of sounding cliché, the work we do together is about building a relationship with your body, mind, and soul. Just as *Fall in Love with the Whispers of Your Heart* has inspired the curiosity of why you respond the way you do, Lux Eterna Healing continues the journey and adds me as a witness and guide. Together we heal what blocks the light of your soul.

For more information about Lux Eterna Healing, go to www.LuxEternaHealing.com

About the Author

Ever since I was a little girl, I enjoyed using my hands to create what I saw within. I loved to color, draw, and write. Once I was introduced to the piano in 5th grade, I was hooked. I had another opportunity to express what was inside using my hands. I had little awareness of how important it was going to be to create and express what was within me.

I went on to get two degrees in music, an undergraduate degree in music education with piano emphasis and a Master's degree in collaborative piano. I loved the creative process, exploring what was behind the notes on the page. It continues to feed my soul.

After my divorce in 2006, I was drawn to the world of Reiki and crystals. Using my hands to create took on a whole new meaning. I could help create balance and healing within a body. I immersed myself in training: Reiki attunements, Munay-Ki Rites, weekly crystal classes, getting certified as a teacher of crystal healing and graduating from the Free Spirit School of Integrated Energy Healing-Developing Consciousness Program.

It is an honor and a blessing to continue to create with my hands: this book, my healing practice through Lux Eterna Healing, and concertizing at the piano. I am grateful for the journey we all share, embracing being the student as much as being the teacher.